The Right to Hope

The Right to Hope
Crisis and Community

by Melvin Rader

University of Washington Press
Seattle and London

Library of Congress Cataloging in Publication Data

Rader, Melvin Miller, 1903–1981
   The right to hope.

   Includes index.
      1. Civilization, Modern—1950–   —Addresses,
   essays, lectures.   2. Hope—Addresses, essays,
   lectures.   3. Community—Addresses, essays,
   lectures.   I. Title.
   HM101.R24   909.82   81-51284
   ISBN 0-295-95836-7   AACR2

For
Virginia
my dear companion

Publisher's Note

The Preface to *The Right to Hope* was the last piece Melvin Rader wrote for publication before his death on 14 June 1981. He had made final corrections to the manuscript of the book and had approved the printer's sample pages, but the galley proofs arrived a week too late for him to check. The title he chose for the book, expressing the enduring optimism reflected in these essays, was given a special poignancy by his tenacious struggle against incurable illness throughout the period when he was collating and editing them. The essays were written over a span of more than thirty years, but their message—as he told his publisher a few days before he died—is more urgent today than ever before.

Contents

Preface

This is a collection of closely related essays. All are concerned with the crisis of world civilization, with the right to
hope that the crisis can be resolved, and with the meaning of
community as the object of hope. More than any of my books
or other publications, they represent the central thrust of my
ideals. While they characterize the general meaning of *crisis*,
the reasons for *hope*, and the ideal of *community*, they apply
these concepts to science, technology, art, religion, and social
theory and behavior. The argument would be too unfocused if
these pervasive themes did not give it a sharp edge.

By *crisis* I refer to no remote historical circumstances, no
small and local disturbances, but to a wide and sustained
period of danger and suspense. Arnold Toynbee similarly uses
the concept of a "time of troubles" in characterizing the great
civilizations of the past. My use of crisis is as broad except that
I focus on the crisis of the late twentieth century. The crisis in
our time is unique in embracing the whole earth and all its
peoples, including their various spheres of culture. In chapter 2 I have tried to analyze the meaning of crisis in these very
inclusive terms, but the idea of world-crisis runs like an obbli-
gato through all the essays.

Without blinking the extreme gravity of the crisis or the
riskiness of historical prophecy, I have tried in my title essay
to defend "the right to hope." Adapting a famous argument of
William James, I contend that hope in the human prospect is

[xi]

far preferable to apathy and despair, because hope and acting on hope are likely to be important means to attaining the prospect hoped for. The affirmative tone is not confined to the title essay. From the earliest to the latest essay, hope thrusts itself upward through my account of the woes of civilized man.

The question inevitably arises, What should be the object of hope? My answer is that neither an acquisitive individualism nor a repressive collectivism will suffice to meet the crisis. A profound restructuring of our social order is necessary, and that restructuring should be based on the ideal of human community.

The meaning of community has been enriched by the thought of many philosophers. I am indebted to Immanuel Kant, Josiah Royce, John Dewey, George Herbert Mead, Ludwig Feuerbach, and Martin Buber. Both an *inner* and an *outer* meaning of community emerges from their reflections. The inner meaning is an appreciation of the uniqueness and intrinsic value of the human person. The spirit of community is realized only when each person regards the other as an end-in-himself, not as a means only. In a real community the means-relation of master to instrument is subordinated to the ends-relation between persons. In this relation no one stands apart from another human being in order to manipulate or exploit him. Each person's essential being is in sympathetic contact with another person's essential being, not as an *object* but as a *presence*, not as a *type* but as an *individual*. The relation is reciprocal: I not only give but receive; I not only speak but listen; I not only respond but invite response. The I is constituted and remade in this relation of reciprocity. In my final chapter, "Crisis and the Spirit of Community," I explore the religious basis of community.

The outer meaning is no less essential than the inner. People often change their minds by changing their circumstances, and change their circumstances by changing their minds. Hence community is realized not in minds alone but in institutions and social structures. We must neither shun all governmental initiatives nor neglect the life-and-death issues of world order. But we *must* insist that social policy—be it political or educational, technological or cultural—should strengthen the freedom and fellowship of individuals and cooperative groups. Ideally, social policies should not be imposed repressively by an élite but should arise spontaneously within an educated and democratic citizenry. This is the outer meaning of community—a meaning which is clarified especially in my fifth chapter in the discussion of John Dewey. As an alternative to the excesses of individualism or collectivism, community in both its inner and outer meaning is the "third way" as yet largely untried.

I have added an Epilogue consisting of quotations that point up the meaning of the book. Among the selections quoted is an eloquent passage from Bertrand Russell in which he depicts the choice between death and life for all humanity. The way of death, if that be the choice, need not be immediate. The finis might not be before the twenty-first century. But finis it will be if nations persist in their folly: the reckless exhaustion of nonrenewable sources of energy, such as fossil fuels and metals; the expansion of population beyond the capacity of the "good earth" to nourish and sustain it; the pollution of land, water, and air with the poisonous wastes of our industrial civilization; the sacrifice of human rights to the inhumanity of dictatorships and bureaucracies; the megalomania of piling up lethal weapons beyond all reason.

In the words of Hobbes: "In all times, kings, and persons of sovereign authority, because of their independency, are in continual jealousies, and in the state and posture of gladiators; having their weapons pointing, and their eyes fixed on one another; that is, their forts, garrisons, and guns upon the frontiers of their kingdoms; and continual spies upon their neighbors; which is a posture of war" (*Leviathan*, 13). After three centuries of ever more destructive weapons, Hobbes's observation is still true. The nuclear holocaust, nevertheless, may even now be postponed, and the "advanced nations" may enjoy a limited joy ride at the cost of future generations. But the last good hope will disappear if this be the ultimate choice. I have tried to depict a "third way" that is the opposite of all this folly. Its core is community in both its inner ethos and its institutional manifestations.

The essays in which these doctrines are expressed have been partially incorporated in two of my later books, but the meaning of the quoted passages has been greatly enhanced by their transfer to the present context. Here the essays are reproduced whole and not in truncated form. Typographical errors in the originals have been corrected, and minor modifications in subheads, footnotes, and the like have been made for typographical consistency. Otherwise nothing has been changed from the original texts except the elimination of a few repetitions and out-of-date remarks. Some repetitions still remain but their omission would impair the continuity of particular passages. Inevitably each essay bears the impress of the time it was written. Obviously, in the earlier essays I cannot refer to persons, events, or publications that emerge later in time. Despite these differences and the wide span of years during which these essays were written—1946 to 1980—they form a coherent body of thought. The issues are more urgent than ever.

Acknowledgments

I am very grateful to my daughter Barbara and my colleague Paul Dietrichson for their generous help, and to Naomi Pascal for her skilled editorial assistance. My long participation in a university interdepartmental course on "The Modern Cultural Crisis," taught under the direction of Professors Melville Hatch and Howard Nostrand, proved highly stimulating. It would be impossible to make the many acknowledgments to the individuals and books that have inspired me.

Information on original and any subsequent publications of these essays is provided in the headnotes. I should like to express my appreciation to the following for permission to reprint them in this volume: *The Kenyon Review* for "Toward a Definition of Cultural Crisis," copyright © 1947 by Kenyon College; The American Association for the Advancement of Science for "Science and World Community"; the American Society for Aesthetics for "The Artist as Outsider"; the Colorado Associated University Press for "Community in Time of Stress"; and the American Philosophical Association for "Crisis and the Spirit of Community." I should also like to thank the following for permission to reprint copyrighted material: Penguin Books Ltd. for the excerpt from *Antigone* from Sophocles, *The Theban Plays*, translated by E. F. Watling, copyright © 1947 by E. F. Watling, renewal copyright by E. F. Watling; George Allen and Unwin (Publishers) Ltd., and Simon and Schuster, a division of Gulf and Western Corporation, for the excerpt from Bertrand Russell, *Portraits from Memory*, copyright © 1951, 1952, 1953, 1956 by Bertrand Russell; Holt, Rinehart and Winston for excerpts from my essays in *Ethics and the Human Community*; Prentice-Hall for excerpts from *Art and Human Values*.

Seattle, April 1981

The Right to Hope

Chapter 1

The Right to Hope

*The Solomon Katz Distinguished Lectures in the Humanities
Series lecture, delivered at the University of Washington,
9 October 1980.*

I

History has lent to the old, old question, "What shall we do
to be saved?" a new terrible urgency. No longer is it a question of hell or salvation for the individual soul—the whole of
mankind is in jeopardy.

The present period is not the first time that there have been
premonitions of utter catastrophe. Nietzsche warned repeat-
edly that we live at the crossroads of human history and that
humankind may irretrievably take the wrong path. William
James remarked that scientific-technological man may be like
the child drowning in a bathtub because he has turned on the
water without knowing how to turn it off. Sigmund Freud
wrote in 1930, more than a decade before the atomic bomb,
that "men have gained control over the forces of nature to such
an extent that with their help they would have no difficulty
exterminating one another to the last man. They know this,
and hence comes a large part of their current unrest, their
unhappiness and their mood of anxiety."[1]

---

[1] "Civilization and Its Discontents" in *The Complete Works of Sigmund
Freud* (London: Hogarth Press, 1961), p. 145.

[3]

The Right to Hope

The anxiety has not diminished since Freud wrote these words. Economist Robert L. Heilbroner has said: "The outlook for man, I believe, is painful, difficult perhaps desperate, and the hope that can be held out for his future prospect seems to be very slim indeed. . . . If . . . we ask whether it is possible to meet the challenges of the future without the payment of a fearful price, the answer must be: No, there is no such hope."[2] After reviewing a massive body of evidence, geochemist Harrison Brown has concluded "that industrial societies are really very fragile, complex systems . . . extremely vulnerable. . . . The probability of survival of industrial civilization is very close to zero."[3]

Others have emphasized the ambivalence of the human prospect. We are confronted, they have said, by "the double aspect of things to come." "Everyone sees a dark figure and a bright one simultaneously, both approaching at startling speed," Elias Canetti has remarked. "You may try to cover up one of them so as to see only the other, but both are inexorably there."[4] Norman Mailer has thus characterized the twentieth century: "It was a world half convinced of the future death of our species and yet half aroused by the apocalyptic notion that an exceptional future still lay before us. So it was a century which moved with the most magnificent display of power into directions it could not comprehend. The itch was to accelerate—the metaphysical direction unknown."[5]

The grounds for anxiety—ecological, military, and social—are obvious. Our technology, rapidly consuming the fossil fuels and ores that are its life-tissues, is like a mad cannibal devouring his own flesh. The madness is the more obvious in view of the population explosion. As births soar and resources dwindle, malnutrition in the underdeveloped countries, with

[2] *An Inquiry into the Human Prospect* (New York: W. W. Morrow and Co., 1975), pp. 22, 136.
[3] *The Human Future: The World Predicament and Possible Solutions* (New York: W. W. Norton and Co., Inc., 1978), pp. 10, 220.
[4] *Tagebuch* (Vienna, 1965) quoted by Ernst Fischer in *Art against Ideology* (London: Allen Lane, 1969), p. 42.
[5] *Of a Fire on the Moon* (Boston: Little, Brown and Co., 1969, 1970), pp. 51–52.

all its terrible costs in physical and mental retardation, afflicts more than half of their populations. Even rich America is threatened with dire shortages of resources, while the submerged portion of its population needs vastly more in goods and services than it is receiving. The increase in numbers here and abroad will add its quota of difficulties to the environmental problems: the pollution of air and water, the destruction of forests and grasslands, the extinction of plant and animal species, the erosion and depletion of the soil.

The ecological and demographic crisis is grave, but the gravest crisis of all is the military. World expenditures on armaments exceed the income of the poorest half of humanity. One quarter of the world's scientists are working on weapons and many million men and women in the prime of life are under arms.[6] Locked in bitter conflict, the Soviet Union and the United States have deployed over 50,000 thermonuclear bombs.

The large-scale use of nuclear weapons "would mean certain destruction of a large part of the world, making it unfit for human habitation, with little chance of recovery." No wonder that Victor F. Weisskopf, the eminent physicist whom I am quoting, concludes that the arms race is the "triumph of craziness." The near catastrophe at the Three Mile Island nuclear plant sent chills down the spines of thousands of people. But Weisskopf asks: "What is the so-called 'worst reactor accident' compared to a nuclear war and its irreparable effects on our environment, on our souls, alive or dead, and on our planet as a whole?"[7] Despite these sobering considerations, nuclear

[6] A recent authoritative survey cites the following figures: "World-wide, the men and women in uniform, and the civilians employed by defense ministries or working in military related jobs, now add up to 100 million people, a population as large as the total labor force of Latin America. About 70 per cent of these are in the armed forces" (Ruth Leger Sivard, *World Military and Social Resources* [Washington, D.C., 1979; copyright by World Priorities, Leesburg, Virginia] sponsored by the Arms Control Association, the Rockefeller Foundation, and similar organizations in the United States, Canada, and Great Britain).

[7] "A Race with Death" in his syndicated column, *Seattle Post-Intelligencer*, 28 May 1978.

proliferation, including the build-up of megaton weapons, continues to accelerate. In terms of the scale of possible disaster, the present crisis is incomparably the most serious that humanity has ever faced. The social relations of human beings are also in disarray. Governments seem incapable of managing their economies, humanizing their technologies, and democratizing their bureaucratic structures. The symptoms of psychological strain—the prevalence of crime, terrorism, and other forms of violence; the addiction to alcohol and hard drugs; the incidence of mental disease; the spread of alienation and anomie—are all signs that things are awry. Most insidious of all is the depersonalization that is more or less ingrained in our mechanized civilization. This reached its apogee in the death camps of the Nazi holocaust. The Nazis tattooed every newcomer with a number, and from that moment he lost his "self," his personal identity, and was transformed into a number to be canceled in the gas chamber. When a great civilized nation can fall to such depths, what confidence can we have in the future? Civilization is a crust that breaks under severe pressure.

II

If the human prospect is so precarious, can we hope to meet the challenge of the future? In seeking an affirmative answer, I recall an old saying: "The two enemies of hope are presumption and despair." I shall attack these enemies in defense of hope, but first I shall explain what I mean by presumption and despair.

By presumption I mean jumping to conclusions. Something is taken to be a fact when it is far from certain. I can illustrate by the opinions of H. G. Wells with respect to the human prospect. In a lecture delivered in 1902, he declared: "In absolute fact the future is just as fixed and determinate, just as settled and inevitable, just as possible a matter of knowledge as the past." Wells admitted the bare possibility of worldwide catastrophes, such as a pestilence of unprecedented magnitude or a collision with an astronomical body from outer space. "I do not believe in these things," he said, "because I have come to believe in other things—in the coherence and purpose in the world and in the greatness of human destiny."[8] In old age, Wells was no less presumptuous, but his vision had turned black. "There is no way out or around or through," he declared. "It is the end."[9] Homo sapiens would soon become as extinct as Brontosaurus. Both his early optimism and his late pessimism outran reason and evidence.

His attitude in old age was not only presumptuous but despairful. *Despair*, as I use the term, is not an alternative to presumption, but a form of it. It is the presumption that there is no hope—"no way out or around or through"—when the evidence does not justify hopelessness. Other examples may be cited. Oswald Spengler was despairful in prophesying the fall of our Western civilization. "Only dreamers," he said, "believe that there is a way out. Optimism is *cowardice*."[10] Jacques Ellul, in a profoundly pessimistic book, denied that free individuals or autonomous groups can long withstand the mechanistic trend of technology. "Technique must reduce man to a technical animal" he said, "the king of the slaves of technique."[11] In a similar vein, Roderick Seidenberg asserted: "The hope of retaining the machine while avoiding the consequent mechanization of society is wholly wishful and fallacious."[12] A character in George Orwell's *1984* declared: "If you want a picture of the future, imagine a boot stamping on the human face—forever."

[8] *The Discovery of the Future* (New York: B. W. Huebsch, 1914), pp. 23, 56. This lecture was initially presented at the Royal Institution on 24 January 1902.

[9] *Mind at the End of Its Tether* (London: Didier, 1945), pp. 4, 15.

[10] *Man and Technics* (New York: Alfred A. Knopf, 1932), p. 104. Italics in the original.

[11] *The Technological Society* (New York: Alfred A. Knopf, 1964), p. 138.

[12] *Posthistoric Man* (Chapel Hill: University of North Carolina Press, 1950), pp. 231–32.

III

I am now prepared to state my argument: presumption will blind us, despair will doom us, hopeful action *may* save us. I shall take as the framework of my argument the famous essay by William James, "The Will to Believe." He said in retrospect that a more accurate title of his essay would have been "The Right to Believe," a title similar to mine, "The Right to Hope." Although he was considering the grounds of moral and religious faith, there is a logical structure to his argument that is adaptable to my purpose. Just as he adapted the argument in "Pascal's Wager," so will I adapt the argument in "The Will to Believe."

Let me first very briefly recapitulate his contentions. He asks the question whether belief without proof or evidence is ever justified, and states several conditions for the right to believe. The first condition is that we are confronted by a *genuine* option. James explains: "Let us give the name of hypothesis to anything that may be proposed to our belief. . . . Now, let us call the decision between two hypotheses an *option*. Options may be of several kinds. They may be—1, *living* or *dead*; 2, *forced* or *avoidable*; 3, *momentous* or *trivial*; and for our purposes we may call an option a *genuine* option when it is of the forced, living, and momentous kind." [13] The second condition justifying faith is that we do not have enough reason or evidence to decide which hypothesis is true. The third condition is that the result of believing in one of the hypotheses is to make life substantially better. When all three conditions are satisfied, we have "the right to hope."

I shall cast my argument in the form that James has thus outlined. What is the justification for hope in the human prospect rather than presumption or despair? This question, I shall maintain, poses a genuine option in the choice of attitudes and

[13] *The Will to Believe and Other Essays in Popular Philosophy and Human Immortality* (New York: Dover Publications, 1956), p. 3.

beliefs—an option that is living rather than dead, momentous rather than trivial, and forced rather than avoidable.

An option is *living* if it makes some appeal to us; it is dead if it leaves us cold. Our question is a living option for anyone who cares for himself and others. Seldom has the need to ward off disaster been more pressing, never has the whole world been more threatened. Few are unmoved by the global prospect of overpopulation, few by ecological devastation, few by psychological malaise, fewer still by the hazard of nuclear holocaust. Humanity has never faced questions of more dreadful import.

The option is *momentous*. It may not be momentous for a person who has hardened his heart and closed his mind. Spiritually, he is already dead. For all those who are truly alive, it matters enormously. It matters whether hope is disappearing from the world and an icy solitude of dread is closing around every thoughtful person. It matters not only in objective terms, it matters here and now how we feel, whether we can look forward with joy and confidence to human betterment, or whether we must yield to the death of hope.

Finally, the option is *forced* rather than avoidable. James characterized a forced option as one in which nondecision amounts to decision. Suppose a desperately ill person is considering whether to have an operation that may or may not save his life. He might have any one of three attitudes: belief, disbelief, or nonbelief. In this instance, nonbelief, the failure to decide, is practically equivalent to disbelief because it has the same consequence, namely, avoidance of the operation. The present crisis of humankind is analogous to the crisis of the very ill person. The question is whether anything sufficient can and should be done. Belief may lead not only to a more sanguine state of mind, but to practical steps toward recovery. Disbelief and nonbelief would have the opposite effect: either would forestall any great effort to meet the challenge. So the argument might run.

I have one reservation about accepting it. James interprets nonbelief as practically equivalent to disbelief. In some but not all situations, this is the case. We should still call an option genuine if nonbelief, although different in its effects from disbelief, is similarly disastrous. In my example of a sick civilization, nonbelief might lead to apathy, whereas disbelief might lead to despair. Apathy and despair are different, but neither is an invigorating alternative to hope. As I define a genuine option, it is an inescapable choice between belief, disbelief, and nonbelief when disbelieving and nonbelieving would have grave, but not necessarily identical, consequences. Hope in the human prospect in our age of crisis is one such option. It is living, momentous, and forced—a genuine response to stark, inescapable problems.

IV

The second condition specified by James in justification of faith is that no sufficient evidence or proof is obtainable to confirm or disprove the hypothesis. Knowledge should suffice when it is within our grasp, he maintained, but faith may be the best substitute when knowledge is unobtainable. Similarly, I contend that the human prospect is too uncertain to permit foreknowledge, and that in its absence, hope is justified.

My generation, born early in this century, has witnessed the most surprising cataclysms: two world wars, the worst depression ever known, revolutionary movements of great scope and fury, the crumbling of vast empires, an arms race that threatens universal death and destruction. No one has intended, no one has wanted, no one has precisely foreseen these developments. Lurching from emergency to emergency, this period in history has been accurately called the "accidental century."

Not even social scientists, much less we ordinary laymen, have been reliable in forecasting the future. It is notorious, for example, how much economists disagree in their longer-range predictions. These disagreements are largely the result of the complex and inconstant nature of economic data immersed as

The Right to Hope

they are in the flow of historical time. The problems of the
physical scientist, in contrast, deal with the constancies of
natural law and lie beyond the range of human historical time.
Hence the astronomer, for example, can predict with exacti-
tude the return of Halley's comet.

Pointing out that the economist enjoys no such advantage,
Sir John Hicks, the Nobel Prize winning economist of Oxford
University, has written: "Economic knowledge, though not
negligible, is extremely imperfect. There are very few economic facts which we know with precision; most of the 'macro'
magnitudes which figure so largely in economic discussions
(Gross National Product, Fixed Capital Investment, Balance
of Payments and so on—even Employment) are subject to
errors, and (what is worse) to ambiguities, which are far in
excess of those which in most natural sciences would be regarded as tolerable."[14] These imperfections explain in large
part why so many economic analyses and forecasts have gone
awry. John Kenneth Galbraith goes so far as to say, "All previ-
sion in economics is imperfect."[15]

We are in no better hands if we turn to other social scientists, because they are faced with similar difficulties. If we
compare the prophecies of Herbert Kahn, Paul Ehrlich, and
Daniel Bell, to mention only three, we find the widest dis-
crepancies. The comprehensive survey, World Futures: The
Great Debate, edited by Christopher Freeman and Marie
Jahoda, reports that the leading forecasters are very much at
loggerheads.[16] What each one foresees seems to spring from
his conservative, reformist, or radical predilections rather than
from any scientific insights. If consensus is a mark of scientific
verification, historical prophecy is little more than guess-
work.

Prophecy is especially hazardous in an age of science and
technology. The best argument to this effect has been stated
by Karl Popper. It amounts to saying that the discoveries of
science and the inventions of technology, in their very novel-

---

[14] *Causality in Economics* (Oxford: Basil Blackwell, 1979), pp. 1–2.
[15] *Money* (Boston: Houghton Mifflin Company, 1975), p. 269.
[16] *World Futures: The Great Debate* (New York: Universe Books, 1978).

ty, cannot be anticipated in advance. Popper's summary of the argument is admirably succinct:

(1) The course of human history is strongly influenced by the growth of human knowledge. . . .

(2) We cannot predict, by rational or scientific means, the future growth of our scientific knowledge. . . .

(3) We cannot, therefore, predict the future course of human history. . . .

The decisive step in this argument is statement (2). . . . *If there is such a thing as growing human knowledge, then we cannot anticipate today what we shall know only tomorrow.*[17]

This argument is applicable to both pure science (know-what) and technology (know-how).

It might be replied that the technological application of scientific knowledge *can* be foreseen. On the basis of such knowledge, for example, Einstein persuaded Roosevelt to embark on the atomic bomb project. But cautious and qualified though his prediction was, it became possible only when its scientific foundation had been laid. No one in the nineteenth century, Karl Marx no more than John Stuart Mill, could anticipate the unlocking of nuclear power. Even when some technological application can be judged a possibility, much additional research and development may be required to make sure. A great deal is known about the hydrogen atom, but no one can know without further research and invention whether its stupendous power can be tapped to meet our energy needs.

When the first atomic bomb was exploded in the New Mexico desert, the immediate thought of Robert Oppenheimer was a line from the *Bhagavad-Gita* (he could read the original Sanskrit): "I am become death, the shatterer of worlds." We have yet to see whether the release of atomic power will be as world-shattering in its ultimate effects as Oppenheimer feared; but this we already know—it has changed the whole

[17] *The Poverty of Historicism* (Boston: Beacon Press, 1957), pp. ix–x. Italics in the original.

moral complexion of our world and its unpredictable effects stretch on beyond the historical horizon.

The *initial* consequence of an invention such as the atom bomb may be foreseen, but not the long and complex chain of consequences stretching far into the centuries. Fundamental technological breakthroughs—such as movable type, the mechanical clock, the telescope and microscope, gunpowder, the steam engine, power loom, airplane, telephone, the discovery of bacteria, the motion picture, electric light, vitamins, television, contraception, nuclear fission and fusion, the transistor, laser, nucleic acid (DNA)—these and other inventions and discoveries trigger innumerable repercussions and consequences beyond the capacity of anyone to foretell. Popper, therefore, did not exaggerate the unpredictability of scientific-technological advances and their innumerable consequences.

His argument is peculiarly relevant when science and technology are the driving forces of the age. So it is at present. The inability to cope with the revolution in technology is the main cause of the human predicament. Technology, like a hare, has raced far ahead, while some other human functions move tortoise-slow. We have split and harnessed the atom, we have hurtled our rockets into the far regions of space, we have plundered nature's treasure house of fossil fuels and ores, we have invented the most cunning machines; but we have not learned how to curb human aggression. Vast, impersonal, bureaucratic organizations, spearheaded by the technologies of communication and management, have developed with dramatic swiftness, while the values and institutions of the free community have in no way kept pace. Our "progress" has been far swifter in the techniques of homicide than in the arts of peace. Cursed by the anachronisms of war and class, this century has been a period of hypercrises. How to eliminate the anachronisms and bring the fast and slow variables into balance is itself a formidable problem in social science and technology.

What hope is there for the human race? The answer as well as the question is directly related to the growth of human knowledge. It will require a wise use of technology to remove the effects of an unwise use. For example, the replacement of the internal combustion engine by an energy-economizing and nonpolluting substitute is needed to alleviate the energy crisis and to stop the fouling of the atmosphere. The discovery of ways to produce and conserve energy, ways to grow and distribute food, ways to check the population explosion, and ways to humanize the organizational structure are required to resolve the crisis.

I do not mean to suggest that the entire cause and cure of the human malaise are science and technology. The highly technical societies could gain immeasurably by recalling the primordial values of human life. They would learn that mechanical civilization, by itself, is quite insufficient to make men happy. They would discover the need to sink their roots deep in the contexts of humanity, and to subordinate matter to life, the mechanical to the organic, the egocentric to the communal. Although more is required for a good life than science and technology, Popper's argument carries a great deal of weight in a scientific and technological age.

There are other reasons for concluding that historical prophecies must be taken with many grains of salt. Bias, which no one can entirely escape, is likely to twist our expectations. The "accidents" of history, such as the assassination of President Kennedy, cannot be foretold. The uniqueness of each historical personage, such as General De Gaulle or the Ayatollah Khomeini, escapes the statistical net of the forecaster. If there is a free-will response to historical challenges, we cannot know in advance how human beings will respond. Forecasts made by projecting present trends into the future may be justified as a warning; they are not justified as a prophecy. So, for example, the French discovered after building the Maginot Line—fortifications suitable to the trench warfare of the 1914–18 period, but utterly inadequate against the blitzkrieg. The late twentieth century appears to be a time when many important trends will change direction. If so, the single-forecast practice based on extrapolating present trends may prove to be terribly costly. It is far less realistic than the hope that envisages alternative possibilities and links morale to transformative action.

Of course some expectations are reasonable—otherwise we could not live from day to day. We have little doubt that we shall wake up tomorrow and find our surroundings much as we would expect them to be. But we should have no such confidence in large-scale and long-range historical prophecies. We can *hope*, we cannot *know*, that humanity's future will be happier than its past. The course of history is more like the growth of a plant than like the movement of an escalator. As D. H. Lawrence has said: "There is no pulling open the buds to see what the blossom will be. Leaves must unroll, buds swell and open, and *then* the blossom. . . . We know the flower of today, but the flower of tomorrow is all beyond us." [18]

V

We have already considered two conditions that James insists are necessary to justify faith: first, that we are confronted by a genuine option between incompatible hypotheses; and second, that there is not sufficient evidence or proof to determine which hypothesis is more probable. If these two conditions are satisfied, the third becomes relevant, namely, that faith in one of the hypotheses will make life substantially better. All three conditions are applicable to hope as much as to faith.

Hope in the human prospect is both reasonable and salutary. We do not *know* that humanity will surmount its crises, but we have ample reason to hope. Human societies have not only survived their time of troubles—they have rallied and leaped to new heights. Some civilizations have been crushed and have sunk fruitlessly to their death; but others have summoned the strength to meet the challenge, and in the act of struggle have achieved a kind of rebirth. The difficulties that now confront humanity provide a superlative challenge to the creative energies of our age. What the final result will be no

[18] *Selected Essays* (Harmondsworth, Middlesex: Penguin Books, 1956), pp. 91–92.

one can foretell, for "the outcome of an encounter cannot be predicted and has no appearance of being predetermined, but arises, in the likeness of a new creation, out of the encounter itself." [19]

The most striking recent evidence of human resilience is the recovery from World War II. The most heavily bombed cities, such as Warsaw, Munich, London, even Hiroshima, snapped back with amazing rapidity. Economies that were reeling, nations near exhaustion, cultures sinking to the level of barbarism, displayed a power of resurgence that confounded the pessimists.

On a much smaller scale, a number of cities in the United States have proved their capacity to recover from peacetime crises. The citizens of Seattle, for example, have saved Lake Washington from irretrievable pollution. They created a public policy committee, adopted a daring program for hygienic disposal of domestic and industrial waste, floated a bond issue, and formed a new metropolitan government to carry the plan to a triumphant conclusion. Likewise, Pittsburgh, once so ugly and polluted that Charles Dickens called it "hell with the lid off," has been greatly improved by its civic leaders and aroused citizens. I need not multiply examples—there are many instances that will occur to you.

Remembering such examples, we should not feel hopeless about the future. The most plausible image of the human prospect is "the double aspect of things to come" suggested by Canetti—we see "a dark figure and a bright one simultaneously, both approaching at startling speed." If a sufficient number of human beings act with wisdom and determination, the dark figure will fade and the other will glow more and more brightly.

What difference does it make whether our response is one of hopelessness or hope? It makes a lot of difference. In the struggle to meet the challenge, hope is our helpmate and loyal

[19] Arnold Toynbee, *A Study of History* (New York: Oxford University Press, 1934), Vol. III, p. 301.

companion, hopelessness is a deserter and turncoat. The death of hope may take the form of either apathy or despair. The former deadens the spirit and freezes the will—it is a failure of nerve. The latter leads to paralysis or desperation, either of which can be fatal.

The tendency of hope and hopelessness to be self-fulfilling prophecies is illustrated by the venture of marriage. The question naturally arises whether a newly married couple will be happy and stay together. Hope helps to create a relation of joy and confidence that ensures, or helps to ensure, the success in marriage that is the object of hope. Hopelessness has the opposite effect: without hope, the marriage is doomed. Whenever, as in this example, the outcome of an endeavor depends on morale, hope helps to ensure success, hopelessness to spell defeat. This is as true in the effort to cope with the human crisis as in any other instance. If the prevailing sentiment is hopelessness, the outlook is dismal. All the forces that tend toward disaster will go unchecked.

I can imagine someone objecting: What has this to do with me as an individual? Why should I bother about evils that I can't prevent? What if millions do suffer from hunger or die in poverty? What if new terrible dictators do arise? What if dissidents are imprisoned or disappear when they speak loudly about the rights of man? What if a nuclear holocaust drives humanity back to the Stone Age? I am willing to talk about these possibilities over a cup of coffee, but I can't do anything about them. It is better for me to enjoy life while I can and let others worry about these global concerns.

The objection is seductive and not easily refuted. It touches on the moral question of selfishness and unselfishness and the practicality of individual action when very large issues are at stake. I have space for only a few words in reply.

Although I have been discussing crises that only a mighty collective effort can resolve, a collectivity has no power to act apart from the individuals that compose it. A race, a class, a state, a nation, a corporation or bureaucracy is not a substance with a mind and will of its own. It is made up of persons in social relations, and it acts only in and through these persons. A great collective enterprise, such as the defeat of the Nazis in World War II, could never have succeeded if each person cared only for himself. The future of our whole civilization depends likewise on you and me and others like us—on millions of *individual* human beings. To neglect our civic opportunities and rely on a bureaucracy is the height of irresponsibility.

Self-realization as well as social fulfillment require that the individual overstep the boundaries of selfhood. Every person feels a kind of double bind: he experiences the entrapment of being confined within his own skin and limited by his individual ego, and yet, like a shipwrecked Robinson Crusoe, he yearns to escape from the little island of his selfhood. He feels obligated to others because he is part of a larger whole, and he cannot deny the claims of morality without crippling this wider self. "He who walks a furlong without sympathy," wrote Walt Whitman, "walks to his own funeral dressed in a shroud."

I do not suggest that there is a perfect coincidence between the good of oneself and the good of others. In a bad social order, such as Nazi Germany, a kind man is likely to suffer more than an unkind. Even in the best of societies, a person may have to choose between his own good and the common good. His sacrifice will be morally justifiable if the social good to be gained by his action, objectively viewed, is greater than the value to be surrendered by the self. More often the deeper good of the individual and the good of society coincide.

VI

I have now adapted the three propositions of James in the defense of hope. First, to embrace hope rather than hopelessness is a genuine option—living, momentous, and forced. Second, we do not possess enough reason and evidence to replace hope with foreknowledge. Third, we have the right to hope because it is vastly preferable in itself and in its consequences to apathy or despair. In *form*, my argument is parallel to that of James, but in *content*, it is very different. I have transposed his argument from the religious to the historical plane, and in doing so I have changed its basic thrust. His essay is akin to Kant's moral argument for religious faith. Kant thought that the great question of religion is "what may we hope," and James similarly defined the essence of the religious hypothesis as "the affirmation that all is *not* vanity." Although both he and Kant believed that the religious hypothesis can be neither proved nor disproved, they thought that we are justified in basing our lives on it. I shall not attack or defend them in their religious options, but I shall point out some crucial differences between their affirmations and mine.

Faith has nothing to do with the *logical* justification of their beliefs. Neither philosopher could argue that his faith in God would ensure, or help to ensure, God's existence. The truth or falsity of such metaphysical beliefs depends upon objective factors, independent of how one feels or thinks. Quite different are those instances in which morale is a major factor in making hope or faith come true. The proposition that we have been considering, namely, that hope in the human prospect is justified, belongs in this latter class. If human beings resolutely hope that the crisis can be surmounted, and if they express that hope in wise and vigorous action, there is a good chance that they will be right. My argument is stronger than that of Kant or James because it avoids shaky theological assumptions and strengthens morale when it helps to make the hope come true.

Moreover, my concern with the human prospect is social; the concern of James, in contrast, is personal, individualistic. "The pivot around which the religious life . . . revolves," he declared, "is the interest of the individual in his private personal destiny." Although wary of religious orthodoxy, James believed "that we can experience union with *something* larger than ourselves"—a cosmic spiritual force—"and in that union find our greatest peace." Here, he speaks of "we," but it is "I," the individual, that is uppermost in his thought. "The axis of reality," he asserts, "runs solely through the egotistic places."[20]

Whatever may be the merits or demerits of this ego-centered religion, it is not what is needed to meet the global crisis of the late twentieth century. Mankind is now required to make the most difficult of transitions—the shift from egocentricity to self-transcendence and community. The object of concern must be the historical future, not the vicissitudes of the solitary individual, nor times past and worlds supernatural, but the *human* world and its prospects. Although we cannot foresee the future, we are not helpless. We can envisage possible scenarios, we can widen and enrich these possibilities, and we can by our choices and endeavors increase the likelihood of some alternatives and the unlikelihood of others. This freedom of action, hedged though it be, can lend a majestic significance and purposiveness to our lives.

The link between action and hope is the theme of a final interview with philosopher Jean-Paul Sartre, who died April 15, 1980. The reflections of this great man on the plight of mankind were still tinged with pessimism. "Despair returns to tempt me again," he said, with the thought that the "third world war . . . is going to break out one day" and human life will end in disaster. Starvation is spreading, "the Cold War seems to be coming back to life," and "the invasion of Afghanistan is a particularly troubling fact." Nevertheless despair must be resisted, hope must be unflagging, and the link between action and hope must be strengthened. "I do not think," he said, "that this hope is a lyrical illusion; it is in the nature of action itself." Hence the mandate of survival is clear: "It is necessary to create a foundation for hope" in morally responsible action.[21]

[20] *The Varieties of Religious Experience* (1902; reprint ed., New York: Doubleday, 1978), pp. 480, 515, 490.

[21] "Today's Hope: Conversations with Sartre," by Benny Levy, in *Telos* (Summer 1980).

The Right to Hope

I conclude that all of us have the right to hope, because without hope we cannot fulfill ourselves as persons or realize our civic duties. "In the way of acting," as Sartre concluded, "there is always hope." [22] We live by hope; without it we lack the will to survive. It is folly, it is spiritual suicide, to give way to presumption or despair. We should resist these enemies of hope with all our might.

[22] Ibid.

Chapter 2

Toward a Definition
of Cultural Crisis

*This essay was written for an interdepartmental course en-
titled "The Modern Cultural Crisis." It was published in*
Kenyon Review *vol. 9, no. 2 (Spring 1947). Much of the essay
was later incorporated into* Ethics and the Human Community *(New York: Holt, Rinehart and Winston, 1964).*

I

In recent years, the word *crisis* has been on everybody's
lips, but there has been little attempt to analyze its meaning.
Since so important a concept requires clarification, the present
article is an attempt to clarify its import. Although I shall seek
to define the *general* meaning of cultural crisis, I shall use as
illustration mainly the contemporary world crisis, partly because it is a good example and partly because it is of intense
concern to us today. I assume that it is unnecessary to argue
that the world is in a state of crisis, and that the time of danger
and tribulation through which we have been living did not
suddenly terminate with the capitulation of the Axis at the end
of World War II.

When in the present context I speak of a *culture*, I am employing the term as the anthropologist customarily employs it
as denoting not just a few of the activities of a society but the
entire range of its activities, conceived as a more or less sys-

tematic whole. In employing culture in this sense, I do not mean that every crisis is total in penetrating all the activities of a society. Indeed, most crises are partial and restricted. There may be a crisis in art, for example, that has very little if any effect upon politics or economics. Moreover, I do not mean to imply that the severity of a crisis is directly proportionate to its extent. A restricted crisis may be much more severe than an extensive crisis. An intense disturbance *tends* to be pervasive but is not necessarily so. However, the great crises of this century, manifested in two vast wars and a tremendous economic depression, have been both very severe and very comprehensive. For the first time in history almost the entire globe has been engulfed in catastrophe and few phases of culture have been immune from the shock.

I shall begin by dismissing two misconceptions. The first is that crisis may be identified with such evils as poverty, disease, and injustice; and the second is that crisis necessarily occurs whenever there is rapid transition. In discussing these views, I shall at the same time indicate certain features of a sounder interpretation.

First, crisis is not to be equated with mere suffering, such as poverty and disease. A primitive society, for example, may be poor and wretched but no crisis can be said to exist if it is making full use of the limited techniques and resources at its disposal. Nor is economic exploitation, with its accompanying injustice and conflict, necessarily a sign of crisis, because exploitation is endemic to any higher type of civilization based upon an economy of scarcity. Nor is widespread disease a mark of crisis if the science of medicine has not developed far enough to eliminate it. When such evils, in view of the technological backwardness of society, are inevitable, they are not a sign of crisis.

Until recently these evils were inevitable. During four thousand years of civilization, the useful arts stagnated, relatively speaking, because the techniques of invention were not sufficiently advanced. In the age of Pericles or Queen Elizabeth or even Napoleon, it was technically *impossible* to maintain a leisure class, necessary for the cultivation of the arts, sciences, and social amenities, without subjecting great masses of human beings to penury and excessive toil. But such evils become indicative of crisis if they reach abnormal and unnecessary proportions. My point is that exploitation, conflict, disease, and poverty—weaknesses never wholly transcended in past history—are signs of crisis at certain times and not at others. Crisis in the society occurs when the *amount* of misery, injustice and conflict is no longer reasonably well adjusted to the potentialities of the economy.

Reasonable adjustment or *maladjustment* must be regarded as relative to the potentialities present at any given historical stage. The vast amount of *unnecessary* poverty, illness, and injustice in our technologically advanced society is a sign of crisis, since it involves a wide disparity between potentialities and achievements, and indicates that some fetter is holding our productive potentials in check. The same amount of suffering at a more primitive stage of society would have to be regarded as normal, since at *that* level, poverty and suffering must be widely prevalent even if the achievements fully measure up to the potentialities of the culture.

I am implying that an essential mark of crisis is the fettering of a culture's potentialities, so that it is wasting or misdirecting its creative capacities. The essential mark of a satisfactory equilibrium, on the other hand, is the relative absence of such waste and misdirection combined with a tendency in the entire culture to enlarge its creative capacities and transform itself by unceasing growth.

I mention the factor of growth because I wish to eliminate a second misconception of crisis. It is possible to confuse crisis with rapidity of transition; and indeed there is a modicum of truth in this point of view, because crises tend to occur during periods of swift change, as for example in the transition from feudalism to capitalism. Yet surely rate of change is not a sufficient criterion of crisis. The Dutch historian, Jan Huizinga, remarks that, because of the increasing acceleration of history, the process of change is much more rapid now than during the crisis and downfall of Roman civilization: "Years seem to have replaced centuries as the yardstick of development." This fact, taken by itself, does not prove that the crisis of Roman history was relatively superficial and that our own crisis is relatively profound.

Rapid transition is not necessarily indicative of crisis because *quantity* of change is less significant than *quality* of change. It makes a deal of difference whether the culture is heavenbent or hellbent. Conservatives, since they tend to prefer the static to the dynamic, often neglect this fact: they habitually regard a rapid rate of change as evil, and therefore as a mark of crisis. The conservative sentiment that order is heaven's first law, however, is less wise than the old adage that to conserve one must reform. In addition to order, consequently, there must be an element of *adventure* in the good life—a moving equilibrium which creatively resolves conflicts by broadening and deepening the order. Especially at the present time, when our civilization has proved so monstrously defective, we need a social outlook that is experimental.

Rapid transition, if it results from good will and intelligent foresight, is a sign of health rather than of crisis. *Failure to* make a change, indeed, may deepen and intensify the crisis, since it may increase the disparity between the potentialities and the accomplishments of the culture.

It is not so much change that is indicative or productive of crisis as *unequal* rate of change, with the resultant lack of synchronization between the relatively fast and the relatively slow variables in the culture. The "status quo," in certain fundamental respects, does not change fast enough; and these "lags" act as basic fetters upon development. As a consequence, the potential and the actual, the ideal and the fact, the "ought" and the "is," the ideological verbalization and the actual behavior, are in sharp contrast. To remove the fetters by a thorough reconstruction of the "status quo" is therefore necessary in order to advance to a more complete integration, in which the actual and the potential are no longer fundamentally opposed. Until this reconstruction occurs, very deep and intense conflicts will persist, conflicts between the old and the new, or between the hypertrophied and the atrophied phases of civilization. These conflicts appear in human thought as basic issues, and in human behavior as crime, economic depression, war, and revolution. Within the present century, for example, a terrible world crisis has been produced by a combination of things new and old: by the swift development of superb mechanical efficiency without a correlative growth in morals and social control, by the rapid increase in factual knowledge without an equivalent advance in synthesis and humanistic disciplines, by the enormous expansion of productive capacity without an adequate transformation of class privileges and property relations, by the very rapid development of international mobility, communication, and exchange without sufficient alteration of the institutions and practices of the absolute nation-state. In all these respects, we have been pouring new wine into old bottles. The result has been a great discrepancy between potentialities and accomplishments. At the very time when scientific and material potentialities have increased by leaps and bounds, barbarism and international anarchy have sprung up and multiplied among advanced civilized peoples.

Our concept of crisis begins to emerge. A crisis occurs when a society develops so unevenly as to produce a grave cultural disequilibrium, in which the more static phases act as fetters to prevent the realization of the proper potentialities inherent in the civilization. The existence of these fetters constitutes not merely an evil and a danger but an opportunity—to remove the hindrances and thus to release the potentialities of the society.

II

Crisis may be defined in terms of a number of factors, such as its causes, its formal structure, and its relation to human, natural, and technological resources. I shall begin the task of further clarification by discussing the formal structure of crisis.

In terms of form or organization, a crisis is a highly dynamic condition of disequilibrium. In the absence of clear definition, it may seem that I am exalting equilibrium as an ultimate

ideal, and that the attempt to do so is unwarranted. Perhaps a
society that is always slightly off balance, in which there are
ferments and tensions and conflicts, is "better"—more creative, productive, progressive, less flat and jejune—than a completely equilibrated society. Does not equilibrium imply stasis? Are not "dynamic" and "equilibrium" antinomic terms?
The force of this objection is indicated by the historical
analysis of Arnold J. Toynbee. In his study of twenty-one great
civilizations, he again and again emphasizes "the sin of Idola-
try," i.e., the infatuation with the status quo, with the traditional ideals, techniques, and institutions. As a civilization
declines, it tends to fall into a more and more rigid pattern of
response, and the creativity of its earlier phases is replaced by
a mimetic regimentation enforced by a "dominant minority."
The people, formerly responding flexibly to the inspired lead-
ership of a "creative minority," now settle into a mechanical
routine. The change is symbolized by the replacement of
Orpheus, the poetic and imaginative leader, by Xerxes, "the
drill sergeant with his whip," who enforces a herdlike conformity upon the masses. This gradual setting in of a cultural
rigor mortis is illustrated in Toynbee's pages by many historical examples, such as the self-idolization of Athens as "the
Education of Hellas" in the period of Pericles, or by the more
extreme cultural petrifaction of Sparta.

If it be objected that I am exalting such a mechanical order,
I would reply that I intend no such implication by my use of
the word *equilibrium*, and that an equilibrium may be either
static or dynamic. A static cultural equilibrium does not eliminate all change because every society is in constant flux, but
the changes consist of slight, or limited and temporary, devia-
tions from the *normal* pattern of life. There is no *cumulative*
development bringing about *fundamental* change. For example, after an earthquake, flood, epidemic, or a brief war involv-
ing no very great strain, there is a reaction and a return to a
normal balance of forces. If a culture, changing in this manner,
is so constituted that its component factors are in general har-
moniously coordinated with one another, we can say that it
exhibits a static equilibrium.

The Right to Hope

A dynamic culture, as contrasted with a static, is one in which *cumulative* changes, either progressive or retrogressive, are taking place in important parts of the culture. Thus there is no stable, persisting, "normal" equilibrium; and if we can, under these circumstances, speak of equilibrium, it can be only a *dynamic* equilibrium. Such an equilibrium occurs when *cumulative* and *fundamental* changes take place, yet in balance and harmony with one another, so that, if at any point in time a survey is made, it is still possible to say that the various phases of development are fairly well coordinated with one another, with an absence of costly unresolved conflicts and frictions.

The norm of social health which I am suggesting is dynamic equilibrium. Its loss means a stasis or a crisis, its reestablishment is the proper aim of reconstruction. I am implying that we should hold fast to two concepts and fuse them together. First, we should recognize that society is, or ought to be, a unity. There should be an interaction and reciprocity of parts; there should be a distinctive character attaching to society as a whole; and each part should contribute to, or be governed by, the total design. Such unity results in more efficiency, fewer disastrous conflicts, greater fulfillment. Second, there should be a continuous *process* of social realization, achieving not merely a greater coherence but a greater comprehensiveness and intensity. In this extending and deepening of civilization, freedom is basic: originality, adventurousness, individuality, are no less important than order. Our goal should not be a tidy, rigid, preconceived unity but a rich and changing harmony: a dynamic, unfolding interaction of free personalities.

These two elements, the orderly and the dynamic, should interpenetrate. As in a great work of art, there should be unity and variety, harmony and richness, familiarity and strangeness, repose and stimulation: a harmony in contrariety, a union of opposites. The good society unfolds like a musical composition, with a theme ever varied and enriched. Conflicts, like musical discords, will occur, but they will either be minimal or be resolved into harmony.

If it be objected that "dynamic equilibrium" is merely an

ideal and never an actuality, and that, if crisis means the absence of equilibrium, *dynamic* cultures are always in a state of crisis, I should reply that my terms must be understood in a relative sense, and that certain historical periods exhibit relatively little crisis and relatively satisfactory, although mobile, equilibrium. Admitting the improbability of the full attainment or prolonged maintenance of any such changing equilibrium, it can at least be approached, and the concept of such an equilibrium can be employed as a means of visualizing and measuring a cultural crisis.

To return to our definition, a crisis is a *dynamic* state, but it differs from a dynamic equilibrium in exhibiting *uncoordinated* rather than *coordinated* development. When there is a grave disturbance of equilibrium, such as that the various cultural factors develop at different rates and with slight coordination, there is a cultural crisis. Moreover, in such a dynamic state of disequilibrium, the future is uncertain and men are challenged by danger and opportunity.

This consequence of dynamic disequilibrium was remarked by the ancient Greek physician, Hippocrates, who was the first to introduce *crisis* as a term in medicine. He believed that disease is a state of physical disequilibrium caused by excess or deficiency of certain fluids in the body—blood, phlegm, yellow bile, or black bile. The turning point, when recovery or death hangs in the balance, he called "the crisis": and he believed that a physician should bring all his remedies to bear at this decisive stage. He thus conceived a crisis as not only a present evil but a challenge to action in the light of an uncertain future. It is the point when danger and opportunity are at their maximum.

An analogous theory of social crisis has been advanced by Toynbee. According to his interpretation, a crisis occurs when the relatively stable organization of society is shattered by a severe blow or pressure: the result is a labile condition in which future prospects are ambivalent, hovering between disaster and resurgence. If the society can summon enough energy and wisdom to meet the challenge, the result is a new springtime of culture. Toynbee illustrates this pattern of "challenge and response" with many historical examples, and establishes the fact that crisis has precipitated both the great disasters and the great creative moments in history.

The challenge may arise from either external or internal causes or a combination of both. It may be due to the intrusion of human or natural forces arising *outside* of the society, such as a flood or a military invasion by an external power. On the other hand, the challenge may arise from *within* the society, as in the case of a class conflict, an undermining of faith, or an intellectual schism. Finally, it may result from both internal and external causes, as in the case of France during World War II, when the invasion of Hitler from without coincided with internal stress and weakness. Now that the world is bound together by a close web of interdependence, every major crisis tends to involve the totality of culture, with causes arising from within rather than simply impinging from without.

A very clear example of challenge, with its character of danger and opportunity, is provided by the modern world crisis. Within recent years, the technical instrumentalities of destruction, including the atomic bomb, have attained a sensational efficiency at the very time when the agencies of order and international government seem but frail reeds. In this situation, we recall the remark ascribed to Clemenceau: "The art of massacring human beings is infinitely more easy than that of governing them." [1] Since the time when this remark was made, the first atomic bomb has been dropped on Hiroshima, and danger has been multiplied a thousandfold: the life and death of civilization now hang in the balance. But opportunity has increased likewise: because of new discoveries, we are trembling on the verge of a new industrial revolution which will make the old industrial revolution look petty indeed. Applied science at last makes possible the passage of mankind from the kingdom of necessity to the kingdom of freedom. "Civilizations before us," as Alfred R. Orage has said, "have died in the midst of their ignorance; but our civi-

---

[1] Quoted by William L. Shirer in his syndicated column. "The Great Wide World," *Oakland Tribune*, 29 December 1945.

lization, if it is doomed to perish, will have the evil distinction of dying not only with the cure at hand, but on the eve of such a life as has never been known since the days of Eden."[2] In view of these developments, we can say that the future will probably be very much better or very much worse than the past. Yet the challenge of such an ambivalent prospect, although magnified by the powers of modern technology, is characteristic of every crisis situation, old or new.

A crisis, to return to our definition, is a highly dynamic condition of disequilibrium characterized by danger and opportunity. At the present historical moment, a precarious equilibrium has in some measure been regained, and to this extent the crisis has abated; but because the development of technology has so far outstripped the arts of government, the crisis threatens to break out afresh in an even more virulent form than before.

III

The opportunity that a crisis presents is based upon the discrepancy between potentialities and achievements. What is being achieved falls far short of what might be achieved. There is some fetter that is holding the potentialities in check, with the result that there is a nonuse or misuse of resources. Hence there is the opportunity to remove the fetter and to realize the potentialities of the society.

The terms which I am employing, *potentiality, fetter, nonuse* and *misuse,* require further clarification. By potentiality, I mean a *developed capacity* that has not yet found its proper use. I do not mean a mere privation—a bare absence of a characteristic. To return to my earlier illustration, the absence of technological development in a primitive society is a mere privation, but millions of idle men and machines, in a period of economic depression, represent developed but unused capacity—something quite different from bare privation.

[2] *Political and Economic Writings* (London: George Allen and Unwin, 1936).

I have said that a prime mark of crisis is the nonuse or misuse of such developed capacity. Let me illustrate. Imagine a young German student just entering college during the late period of the Weimar Republic. He is trying to decide upon a career. "I wish to be a doctor," he announces. "Sorry. There are already too many doctors," is the immediate response. "I wish to be a teacher, then," the young man declares. "Too bad. There are already more teachers than can find employment," is the inevitable answer. "Well then, I would like to be an engineer," the student insists. "Sorry again. There is no longer any demand for engineers," his advisors reply. Whatever profession the young man considers, he is at once greeted by the response that professionals of that type are too numerous. This situation is a sign of crisis because it indicates that there is a gross failure to employ the human and technical resources of the society.

Now let us imagine the same student a few years later. There is no longer any question of unemployment. He is busy, extremely busy, and as a youth leader in the Nazi movement, he has a vocation which he can call his own. He and his fellows are intensely occupied burning books, baiting Jews, liquidating liberals and radicals, preparing for war. We can no longer speak of nonuse of capacity (except among the Jews, liberals, and radicals) but surely we can speak of misuse; and we can say that the society is still in a condition of crisis, which is even more intense than before.

But now we have introduced a normative concept. How shall we define misuse and how shall we conceive of *proper use*? This question may be answered either in terms of standards relative to the culture or in terms of more universal standards. From an abstract, absolute standpoint, societies almost never make a very "proper use" of their productive potentialities. Thorstein Veblen, in his *Theory of the Leisure Class*, pointed out that "conspicuous waste," with a consequent failure to produce and consume for basic biological human needs, is a general characteristic of human culture. More recently the American anthropologist, Melville Herskovits, has remarked that in every society of which we have knowledge, there is organized ceremonial waste, often on a great scale. From the standpoint of cultural relativism, this uneconomical lavishness in consumption and honorific destruction of property are not signs of crisis unless they are "abnormal"— unless they considerably exceed the limits deemed "reasonable" by public opinion in that community. When a certain primitive Melanesian tribe, for example, deliberately destroys a large crop of yams for ends deemed moral or religious, this behavior is not a sign of crisis, since it is a characteristic and socially approved feature of their culture. In contemporary America, the wasteful standards of the leisure class, or the immense amount of waste normally associated with advertising, is not a sign of crisis, because, given the mores of our business civilization, such waste is considered normal and even proper. But the waste involved in a vast depression or a world war *is* a sign of crisis because it is not accepted as reasonable and necessary by the conscience of the community, or at least by a very large obstreperous class within that community. We can thus define proper or improper use of resources in terms relative to the mores and public opinion of the given community.

Such a relative standard, however, is not always satisfactory in determining the misuse of resources. If we revert to our previous illustration, the youth leader in the Nazi movement who was burning books, baiting Jews, liquidating liberals, and preparing for war, was *not* engaged in improper activity according to the norms that had become predominant in Germany. Sometimes a society becomes deranged: a "national psychosis" may develop in a frustrated and defeated people. The standards relative to such a society are no longer serviceable in defining the improper use of resources. Unless we are to surrender all rational basis for condemning such a society, we must find an independent and less relative standard.

In formulating such a universalist norm of welfare, it is possible to employ any one of a large number of ethical alternatives. To avoid a long argument I shall simply define human welfare as the satisfaction of wants with the accompanying pleasure; and human misery as the frustration of wants with the accompanying displeasure. Further refinements in analysis are debatable and hardly necessary in the present context. A society from this point of view can be said to function properly if, within the necessary limits of its historical situation, it conduces to the maximum fulfillment of wants, everybody considered and in the long run. The frustration of wants, estimated thus inclusively, is conversely the sign of a malfunctioning society. *Abnormal* waste, measured in terms of such frustration, can then be regarded as a sign of crisis.

Within every society there are forces that tend toward the fulfillment of wants. If the wants remain unfulfilled despite the developed capacity of the society to fulfill them, we can speak of a fetter that is holding the potentialities in check. It would be wrong to suppose that this fetter is simply evil. On the contrary, the analysis of Hegel seems to be basically sound, that the thesis fetters the antithesis, the old fetters the new, the tradition fetters the innovation; and that, nevertheless, the ideal resolution of the conflict is not the cancellation of either set of values but the conservation of both sets through their translation into a more inclusive organization.

A crisis, therefore, is a dynamic state of disequilibrium, in which wants are frustrated, resources are unused or misused, and potentialities are fettered by the disproportionate development of cultural factors.

IV

This definition is abstract; it tells us nothing about the concrete forces of history. To obtain such a relatively concrete interpretation, we must look to the various extant philosophies of history. Should we, for example, with Ellsworth Huntington, emphasize geographical conditions; or with Joseph Arthur de Gobineau, racial factors; or with Carlyle, the role of great men; or with Marx, economic forces; or with Henry Adams, technological development; or with Hegel, ideas and ideologies? Or should we, with Ruth Benedict, content ourselves with a pluralistic view of history, finding merely a variety of causes and cultural patterns? In so brief an article, I cannot essay to choose between these alternatives, but I shall illustrate the meaning of crisis by the example of our present world predicament, with a few side glances at the crises of the past.

It is obvious that we have recently witnessed, in depression and war and cultural barbarism, a prodigious waste and misdirection of material and psychological resources, and the resultant frustration of human wants. Why, in our remarkably well-equipped civilization, has there been such a great discrepancy between potentialities and achievements? The answer, as I have suggested, is to be sought in the disproportionate development of cultural factors resulting in a profound disequilibrium and the consequent fettering of the culture's potentialities by the conflicts between the hypertrophied and the atrophied phases of the culture. Two sorts of uneven development are here to be traced: first, the relatively great development of the privileged classes in society at the expense of the underprivileged; and second, the relative overdevelopment of certain traits at the expense of others.

If we consider the first factor, the disproportionate development of social classes, we are confronted by a division of men into the two "nations," the rich and the poor, and the resulting class conflict. There can be no question about the basic nature of this factor. It is well known that Marx has emphasized it, but it is less well known that Toynbee, basing his conclusions on different premises and a much wider survey of history, has concluded that the unequal development of social classes is a fundamental cause of crisis and cultural disintegration in the twenty-one great civilizations which he surveys. Or to cite a more particular illustration, Michael I. Rostovtzeff, whose knowledge of the classical period is unsurpassed, has concluded that the main cause of the crisis and breakdown of the Greco-Roman civilization was its aristocratic and exclusive nature. The lower classes were subjected to slavery and financial ruin, and this condition was never corrected, despite class war and the shift of power from older propertied classes to new ones. He suggests, in the light of this analysis, that "the evolution of the ancient world has a lesson and a warning for us. Our civilization will not last unless it be a civilization not of one class, but of the masses." Similarly, much of the weakness of medieval civilization, or modern capitalist civilization, is to be traced to class-stratification and the unequal conditions of the many as opposed to the few. But, whereas in past historical periods the productive system was not sufficiently developed to permit a free and ample life for the masses, today an economy of abundance, although it cannot be realized without strenuous effort, is no longer a utopian dream.

Now let us turn to the second kind of unequal development: the disproportionate growth of cultural factors. It is difficult to deny, once the atomic bomb so sensationally emphasized the fact, that technology is the greatest dynamic force in our society, and that failure to adjust our institutions and productive system to this force imperils the whole structure of civilization. This brings to mind the contention of Marx that the forces of production—the techniques and instruments—change more rapidly than the social relations of production—the class-structure and institutions of property; and that recurrent crises are primarily caused by this unequal development. I agree with the Marxian insistence upon the crucial importance of this economic disequilibrium, and I also believe that the most fundamental problem of our civilization is, for the most part, economic: how to achieve a system of *total* production for the maximum satisfaction of human needs. For the sake of a completer interpretation, however, we should generalize the analysis and speak not only of economic but of moral and other sociological factors. We may say that modern technology tends to develop much more rapidly than social control, moral adjustment, and the class structure of society; and the result is a violent disequilibrium. But in stating this view, we should extend the concept of "technique" beyond economics to many fields. In recent years, there have been fundamental inventions, for example, in military and administrative techniques and in the psychological methods of propaganda; and all such inventions disturb the social equilibrium and act as dynamic forces in history. The rise of Hitler was the result of the cunning manipulation of propaganda as well as the result of older types of physical technology. The release of atomic power, although prepared by a great deal of previous research, resulted from the pressure of military exigencies rather than directly from economic motives.

It is well to remember, also, that the very rapid expansion of technology would have been impossible without the swift development of pure science. Is the disequilibrating effect of pure science confined to its influence upon technology? I believe not. The swift pace of scientific discovery, even apart from technology, has had a profoundly unsettling effect upon our modern world-view. New scientific discoveries are made more rapidly than we can spiritually and culturally assimilate them. Confusion results when the new truth, itself too complex and abstruse for the laity to comprehend, supplants the old truth. If once more we seem to be plunged into intellectual night, one reason is that there has been a very rapid increase in factual knowledge without an equivalent advance in synthesis and a sense of values. We therefore lack an adequate spiritual assimilation of scientific ideas and techniques; and our wonderful new resources, for want of this right orientation, are linked to techniques of death rather than to arts of life.

To summarize: the prime mark of a crisis is neither widespread misery nor rapid change, either of which may exist when no crisis is present, but a great discrepancy between potentialities and accomplishments. In terms of *resources*— natural, human, and technological—there is abnormal nonuse or misuse, measured either by a standard relative to the mores and public opinion of the given society, or by the more universalist standard of the frustration of wants. In terms of *organization*, there is a highly dynamic condition of disequilibrium, as a result of which the future is very uncertain and the society is challenged by danger and opportunity. In terms of *causes*, there is the unequal development of cultural factors, the pouring of new wine into old bottles, with a consequent fettering of potentialities by the conflicts and cultural lags which under these conditions appear. By implication, an adequate program of reconstruction must greatly reduce the two main forms of unequal development: the disproportionate development of social classes and the unequal development of cultural aptitudes. In the present critical phase of world history, there should be a very strenuous effort to realize social justice and to cultivate intellectual synthesis, humanistic insight, and social planning, both within and among the nations, so that the vast potentialities of our civilization can be released for human welfare. The task of reconstruction, moreover, should be conceived as the attainment of a new dynamic equilibrium and not the return to a static condition of "normalcy." Lest the old bottles burst with the fermentation of the new wine, we may be forced to prepare the new containers: the profound reorganization of ideals and institutions and human relationships.

Chapter 3

Science and World Community

Published in Scientific Monthly *62 (June 1946): 500–10.*

H. G. Wells once remarked that the fate of the world depends upon a race between education and catastrophe; but in view of the atomic bomb, he has more recently announced that catastrophe is obviously winning, since science and technology are developing more rapidly than man's ability to control them. Others, even more alarmist, have predicted that atomic fission will ultimately set off a chain reaction which will explode the entire planet.

Possibly we can dismiss this particular nightmare but we cannot easily dismiss this *type* of nightmare. Instead of predicting the total destruction of our planet, we may, like Wells, speak of the leveling of civilization in a vast chaos. All that we cherish may be destroyed because man's capacity to make scientific discoveries outstrips his capacity to control them.

Looked at in this context, the question what men shall believe acquires an incredible poignancy. Now as never before we must go back to fundamental questions. What is man—a soul, a mechanism, a psychophysical organism? What is man's place in the cosmos? What is the essential value of human life? What is the nature of the good society? What is the essence and destiny of civilization? Every struggle loses its meaning, every social movement its orientation, unless these questions be faced. Without a world view, strong enough to be the basis of civilization, we cannot substitute reintegration for the disintegration which has been at work for several centuries and which has led great nations into moral and intellectual barbarism. Without a different *sort* of world view than has been prevalent, we cannot make the arts of life prevail over the techniques of death.

It is possible that we shall have to go down to the very bottom of the pit where all faith and reason are lost. But it is a steadying thought that science has vast potentialities for good as well as for ill. Pure as well as applied science can help steady our nerves by giving us a new interpretation of the nature of things.

Apart from its technological applications, science has contributed in two essential respects to the establishment of a better type of civilization: first, in its content and second, in its method. In content, science is providing a new view of the world and man's place in it, a realistic vision which emphasizes the interrelatedness of things and which thereby reinforces the cooperative ideal of human life. In method, science involves a broad community of interpretation, a worldwide fellowship of truth seekers; and it thus prefigures the cooperative organization of mankind. Its proper utilization, moreover, requires a gigantic effort at synthesis, so that the vast and ever-accumulating mass of scientific information can be integrated into a unified interpretation of reality.

As we study contemporary science and the philosophy based upon it, we begin to see an emerging synthesis of thought and action, a possible new basis of civilization. The core of this synthesis is a world view based upon two ideas. First, the world is a complex of interacting processes—everything is relational—nothing exists in bare abstractness, parted off from the rest of existence. Second, the world as evolving has various levels with distinct, irreducible characteristics, such as the mechanical, the organic, the conscious. These two ideas coalesce into a single concept: the evolving multidimensional community of all human beings and, in an infinitely wider compass, of all the interacting entities in the universe.

Admittedly, we are here discussing not the technical con-

tent but the ideological implications of science. The two must
be distinguished. For example, we can distinguish between
the technical content of Newton's astrophysics and the ideological implications which Locke, Pope, Voltaire, the French
physiocrats, and Newton himself read into it. Society will always discover such implications, and we need not regret the
fact. Certainly science is a better foundation than superstition for a comprehensive interpretation of reality. Admitting
that "the new world view" which I shall discuss contains
speculative elements, I believe that it involves no such mis-
reading of science as the supposed implications of Newtonian
physics to which I have just referred.

As far back as the Victorian period, the discovery by Max-
well and Faraday of the electromagnetic field represented a
fundamental departure from the older physical notions of relatively discrete unchanging particles and external relations.
Subsequently, physical scientists have built up a new type of
"field physics" in which atoms or electrons are conceived to
be interdependent events functionally dependent upon their
spatio-temporal environment. As a result of the new concepts
of space-time, of relativity, of quantum and nuclear physics, of
the time and space rate of energy, of Heisenberg's principle of
indeterminancy, the universe depicted by physical science
has become radically different from the "world machine" of
Galileo and Newton. This difference primarily involves the
increased recognition of wholes and integral processes. The
region, the context, the given totality, the space-time configuration, the emerging levels of organization have taken the
place of the old rigid atoms, the empty, featureless space, the
static order of events, the mere positions without contextual
reference.

Similarly in biology there has been an increasing emphasis
upon integral part-whole relationships, upon the idea of the
organism, in which the whole in a sense is prior to and deter-
mines its parts; the idea of the ecological community, in which
organisms socially live and function; and the idea of emergent
stages in evolution, in which there are real creative syntheses
and not mere additive resultants. Psychology has been slower

[41]

The Right to Hope

in responding to formism, but even here there has been an
increasing tendency (represented by many besides the gestalt
psychologists) to think in terms of organic wholes and structural relationships. Likewise in the social sciences there has
been a general revolt against discrete individualism and a
marked tendency to think in terms of interdependence. Modern history and anthropology, moreover, have made us aware
that our competitive economic order is only one among many
historical systems, and that consequently our system is no
more natural or immutable than very different cooperative
systems, which similarly arise and perish. Everywhere in science the old fixed concepts and counters have broken down
and a new world view is emerging.

If we analyze what is involved in this world view, we find
four essential propositions. First, the universe exhibits a
series of levels of increasing complexity and wider integration: electrons, atoms, molecules, simple cells, plants, animals, personalities, human communities. Second, there is a
tendency for these levels to succeed each other in time, the
more inclusive and complex levels emerging at a later stage of
cosmic development; and hence reality is dynamic and evolutionary. Third, the integration also occurs as morphological
envelopes in space: societies enveloping societies which in
turn envelop societies. For example, the body envelops the
organ, the organ the cell, the cell the molecule, the molecule
the atom, and the atom the electron. Fourth, each envelope
and integrative level exhibits its own emergent qualities and
laws. This means that every science has its distinctive
methods and subject matter, corresponding to a certain level
of emergence, so that it is a false reduction to maintain that
sociology is "nothing but" psychology, or that psychology is
"nothing but" physiology, or that physiology is "nothing but"
chemistry, etc.

It follows from these propositions that idealism—the theory
that all reality is mental—is improbable, since mind apparently emerges out of, and is dependent upon, a high level of
biological complexity. It also follows that any *reductive*
mechanism or materialism—the theory that all reality is mere-

ly physical—must be rejected, since biological, mental, and social qualities, with the values and purposes to be found at the higher levels, are quite as indefeasibly real, although not as widely dispersed, as any chemical and physical processes. Thus both a *leveling up* and a *leveling down* interpretation of science and reality must be abandoned in favor of a theory of *distinct, graded, and progressive levels.* Finally, it follows that the world is to be interpreted in terms of a flexible organicism, since nature as a whole exhibits a nisus toward social organization.

A possible objection to the above interpretation is that discrete mechanism never has existed in pure science, and that real scientists have always taken account of systematic wholes, interactive elements, and emergent characteristics. Professor Gustav Bergmann, one of the ablest of the logical positivists, for example, objects to "the exaggerated importance" that the gestalt psychologists such as Leo Wertheimer attach to the idea that a composite effect is not the additive sum of partial effects. He writes:

> What Wertheimer and his students so emphatically assert is essentially this. If C_1 causes E_1 and C_2 causes E_2, then the simultaneous occurrence of C_1 and C_2 does not as a rule cause the occurrence of E_1 and E_2. . . . To give an illustration which is drastic but, I believe, not unfair: a dog which has been appropriately trained runs away from his master when shown a stick and approaches a piece of food held out to him. If both stick and reward are shown to the animal, will it both flee and approach his master? Obviously not, but whoever said it would? . . . There is never any a priori reason to assume that the joint effect will be the logical conjunction of the partial effects. If additivity is the name for such unjustified inference then all empirical laws, whether elementaristic or organismic, are superadditive, and the thesis fights a straw man.[1]

Such criticism is extremely valuable in forcing scientists and philosophers more carefully to define their concepts, but

[1] "Holism, Historicism, and Emergence," *Philosophy of Science* 2 (October 1944):217.

it does not—nor was it intended to—disprove the fact that a fundamental shift in the ideology of science is occurring. I have already distinguished between the *ideology* of science and the *technical content* of scientific laws. Granted that science in its laws has always taken account of the superadditive composition of forces, it remains nonetheless true that ideologically we are shifting to a greater and greater emphasis upon form, pattern, creative synthesis, communal relationships, and total configurations. Even in its strictly technical content, science has been affected by, and has participated in, this shift. The insight that the influence of the whole must be kept in mind in order to explain the character and activity of any actual part has had an increasing effect upon both laymen and scientists, and consequently such fictitious entities as rigid atoms and completely egoistic human beings have been banished to the limbo of superstition. The extent of this shift can be exaggerated, but the shift is indubitable.

Many laymen and some few scientists, however, still interpret plant and animal life almost exclusively in terms of an individualistic struggle for survival. This tendency goes back to fundamental Darwinian concepts: "chance variation," "natural selection," and "survival of the fittest." One of the classic, although inaccurate, interpretations of Darwinism is Thomas Henry Huxley's essay *Evolution and Ethics*, in which "the gladiatorial theory of existence" is presented in terrifying terms. The law of nature, he tells us, is "ruthless self assertion," the "thrusting aside or treading down of all competitors." In this process, the strong and aggressive trample down the weak, and in this sense only do the "fit" survive.

The ethical reactions to this theory differ according to individual predilections. Huxley, for example, believed that man's duty is to maintain, with lonely and pathetic idealism, a Promethean defiance of nature and of nature's laws. "The progress of society," he declared, "depends not on imitating the cosmic process, still less in running away from it, but in combatting it." The more common view was that of Herbert Spencer, who argued that if human beings break with nature, nature will break them. Darwinian concepts, when applied to society, were almost always used to support individualism and predatory behavior: to oppose social humanitarianism and to rationalize war, imperialism, and exploitative capitalism. Even in very recent years, the same point of view has been maintained by Oswald Spengler, with his theory that man is "a beast of prey," and by the fascists, who adapted this doctrine to their own purposes. Hitler declared: "The whole of nature is a continuous struggle between strength and weakness, an eternal victory of the strong over the weak. . . . There is no humanitarianism but only an eternal struggle, a struggle which is the prerequisite for the development of all humanity."[2] In less exaggerated form, the same doctrine has become part of the folklore of American capitalism. "You can't make the world all planned and soft," says the typical businessman of Middletown. "The strongest and best survive—that's the law of nature after all—always has been and always will be."[3]

Since the time of Darwin, however, a vast amount of evidence has been amassed to show that not only struggle but mutual aid is a major factor in evolution. A notable succession of books, such as Henry Drummond's *The Ascent of Man*, André Cresson's *L'Espèce et son Serviteur*, Peter Kropotkin's *Mutual Aid*, John A. Thomson and Patrick Geddes' *Life: Outlines of General Biology*, and Edwin G. Conklin's *The Direction of Human Evolution*, have maintained that parental care, kin sympathy, altruism, and mutuality are potent factors in survival and evolutionary development.

In an article which reviews the evidence, Dr. W. C. Allee, a distinguished American biologist, concludes:

> The picture that emerges from the cumulative studies on social biology is one in which cooperations and their opposite, disoperations, both exist. There are both egoistic and altruistic forces in nature, and both are important. The question arises insistent-

[2] *Hitler's Words* (Washington, D.C.: American Council on Public Affairs, 1944), pp. 3–5.
[3] R. S. and H. M. Lynd, *Middletown in Transition* (New York: Harcourt Brace, 1937), p. 500.

The Right to Hope

ly as to which of these is the more fundamental and potent. . . .
After much consideration, it is my mature conclusion, contrary
to Herbert Spencer, that the cooperative forces are biologically
the more important and vital. . . . Under many conditions, the
cooperative forces lose. In the long run, however, the group-
centered, more altruistic, drives are slightly stronger. If cooperation had not been the stronger force, the more complicated
animals whether arthropods or vertebrates, could not have
evolved from the simpler ones, and there would have been no
men to worry each other with their distressing and biologically
foolish wars.[4]

Allee's careful conclusion is fairly typical of the opinion of
contemporary biologists, who regard the views of Huxley,
Spencer, Spengler, and Hitler as a one-sided exaggeration and
caricature of nature. At the 1940 meeting of the American Association for the Advancement of Science in Philadelphia, there
was a symposium on "Science and Ethics" in which some of
America's most distinguished scientists, including a number
of eminent biologists, agreed that human cooperation is a
more important factor in survival than human competition.
The more sophisticated biologists, moreover, realize that the
life of man in society, although it necessarily rests upon a
biological foundation, exhibits many cultural characteristics
which cannot be reduced to merely biological terms. The
direct study of human society by anthropologists and other
social scientists has proven that "human nature" is remarkably
plastic, and that the highly cooperative society of the Arapesh
in New Guinea, for example, is quite as "natural" as the fierce-
ly competitive society of their near neighbors, the head-
hunters.

In view of the newer trends in both the physical and biological sciences, we can say that our tendencies toward community are as innate and as well founded in nature as any of
our competitive drives; and that our problem is to keep competition in its proper place, directing it toward worthy ends
and subordinating it to, or coordinating it with, the even more

[4] "Where Angels Fear to Tread," Science, 1943, pp. 97, 521.

fundamental tendency toward organic and communal relationships. The most fruitful kind of competition, such as the friendly rivalry of scientists in the discovery of truth, is the sort that contributes to a common cause and that consequently is not an alternative to cooperation but an aspect of it. The change in the ideology of science is correlated with a very profound transition in social thought and action. A new collectivistic order has been growing for many decades within the womb of the old order. We can see the signs of this growth in the social-mindedness of various modern thinkers—for example, in far-seeing economists such as Thorstein Veblen and John Maynard Keynes, in adventurous sociologists such as Patrick Geddes and Karl Mannheim, in influential philosophers such as John Dewey and Alfred North Whitehead. We can see the same trend in the increasing emphasis upon planning, organization, and social control in all of the social sciences. We can discover the signs of transition, sometimes cruel and perverse, in the collectivist revolutions and political upheavals of the modern world.

After considering recent scientific and social tendencies, the English biologist, Joseph Needham, declares:

> It may be that we are on the threshold of a long period, lasting perhaps for several centuries, in which the organic conception of the world will transform society, giving it a unity more comradely and equal than feudalism, but less chaotic and self-contradictory than the centuries of capitalist atomism.[5]

This very interesting sentence requires elucidation. Needham, I am sure, does not mean to imply that "the organic conception of the world" will, in and by itself, transform society. He elsewhere recognizes the decisive role played by economic causes in any such fundamental change. He means that the "organic conception" prefigures and facilitates this profound alteration.

[5] "A Biologist's View of Whitehead," in Paul A. Schilpp, ed., *The Philosophy of Alfred North Whitehead* (Evanston, Ill.: Northwestern University Press, 1941), p. 251.

Also he does not mean to imply that society is a giant organism, a kind of monstrous leviathan with a soul of its own. The term *organic* is so loaded with biological connotations that we must use it with extreme caution in connecting it, as Needham does in this passage, with a human social organization. Society is to be conceived as an integrative structure the members of which are bound together by social relations which determine their essential personalities. Outside of these relations, they would be very different, if indeed they could even exist. Such internal, or essential, relations, as opposed to merely external and inessential, are often called organic, and there can be no valid objection to the term if the reader clearly understands that groups without being literally organisms may have a touch of the organic, some more and some less.

If we are not to misunderstand Needham and to misinterpret the nature of the new scientific "world view," we must recognize that *organic*, as he and I employ the term, must be understood in terms of different grades and types of unity. First, a part may be related to a whole in such a manner that its normal characteristics and activities will remain virtually unchanged whether it is "in" its normal whole or not. An example of a part thus externally related to its "whole" is provided by the archaic conception of a rigid, unimpregnable atom grouped with like atoms in the extrinsic, indifferent receptacle of space and time. Any such whole is a mere aggregate, and no one would call the functional and existential *independence* of its part an "organic" relationship. Second, a part may be related to a whole in such a manner that it undergoes an *internal* change, small or great, when it is isolated. Such *functional dependence*, which admits of infinite degrees from near independence to very close integration, can be called *organic* in the wide and sometimes metaphorical use of the term. Third, a part may be related to a whole in such a manner that it becomes quite unrecognizable, or cannot even exist, when isolated. This *existential dependence* can be called *organic* in the strictest sense of the term. Science is now recognizing that, although some wholes are mere heaps or collections in that they exhibit only the first type of unity, a vast number of wholes, and indeed such fundamental "kinds of things" as atoms, molecules, cells, organs, organisms, minds, and societies, can be fully described only in terms of the *second* and/or *third* types of unity. The increasing emphasis in science and philosophy upon functional and existential dependence constitutes a profound revolution in human thought; and it is this emphasis that I have in mind when I speak of the rise of "a new world view," and that Needham has in mind when he speaks of "the organic conception of the world" that modern science and philosophy have given us.[6]

He is surely right in prophesying a revolutionary change in human thought and institutions. We seem to be involved in the most rapid and profound change that humanity has ever experienced. Some kind of new order, therefore, is inevitable, whether for better or worse; but we can understand its necessities, appreciate its potentialities, and contribute to its values. If we are guided by understanding and motivated by good will, we cannot only mitigate the cruelty of the transition but gradually build a humane and cooperative order. There is nothing, as we have seen, in our scientific understanding of man and his place in the universe that need discourage us in such an attempt. The ideal of a universal human fellowship is based upon the nature of things.

If we turn from the *content* to the *method* of science, we find that it involves, to employ the suggestive phrase of Josiah Royce, "a community of interpretation." To understand what is meant by this phrase, it will be helpful to analyze the nature of ordinary thought.

If we attend to any immediate object of awareness, to *this* patch of color, *this* rustle of leaves, *this* twinge of pain, it is always a particular and private datum: a different impression than appears at any other moment or to any other man. As soon as we *think* about the object, however, we relate it to various other objects: we connect the immediately given with the non-given. "This moment" is identifiable as *this* moment only

---

[6] Cf. Joseph Needham, "Integrative Levels: A Revaluation of the Idea of Progress," *Modern Quarterly* I (January 1938):32–33.

because it stands in contrast to a moment ago which I now remember and the next moment which I anticipate. "This room" means "this" to me only because I think of some other room, and it means "room" to me only because I think of the house and of the fact that this is *a* room: an example of a class, a particular instance of a universal. To sever all such connections would be to render experience meaningless, to eliminate experience at the *human* level of insight. All our thinking, as Kant long ago demonstrated, is thus contextualistic: every object has meaning only through its social relations with other objects.

The context within which an object acquires meaning, moreover, is not merely the individual's private experience but the shared experience of a group of people. Despite the fact that individuals see objects in egocentric perspective, they interpret the objects as the "same" for all perceivers. At dinnertime, you and the other members of your family, for example, believe that you are in the same room and are eating at the same table, and the stubborn privacy of each of your immediate sensations does not prevent the subconscious creation of this community of interpretation. The ordinary objects of touch and sight and sound are regarded as essentially common objects, the "same" for all who experience them, because all of us fit our experiences into the wider social context of group experience, interpreting our private data as "aspects" of a common world. Without collating our experiences with those of others, we could engage in no conversation, no intercourse, no communication of any meaningful kind with other human beings.

Without this social interchange and correlation of impressions, moreover, there can be no meaning attached to the "external world": the environment in which we all move, breathe, and have our being. As Royce pointed out, the only reason we have for supposing that the moon is not just a chimera of private perception, such as "the nonexistent color" seen by the color-blind person, is that others see the "same" bright disc and its effects: it is witnessed by the testimony of innumerable human beings and hence is part of the "real world."

Thus there is a close connection between the quest for truth and the creation of a community. This is the reason why, again and again in the history of human thought, the masters of truth have created a community of "seekers." Pythagoras, Plato, Epicurus, Jesus, Confucius, Buddha, Marx: these are only a few of the men who founded communities for the cultivation of insight. An integral part of the "Socratic method," for example, is inquiry in common among a group of men bound together by love of philosophy and love of each other. If it is no longer necessary for a modern thinker to create a community, it is because science and education as now organized are essentially communal: but the community of learning is as yet embryonic and needs to be nourished.

Science is essentially a community of interpretation when elaborated systematically and critically. The effort of science is primarily *to connect:* it is concerned with the whence and the why and the whither of things; with the causal relations of an object with a great many other objects in the universe. In elaborating its web of causal connections, science makes use of hypotheses which become established theories when verified. The degree of verification increases when the theory unites a greater number of relatively independent data, when it is, in this manner, both coherent and comprehensive. Newton's mechanics gains immensely in cogency when it not only serves to unify the area of mechanics but the hitherto unrelated area of astronomy. Darwin's theory of organic evolution similarly acquires strength when it not only unifies the data of paleontology but the previously independent data of embryology. Thus the method of science, like the method of common sense, is *contextualistic:* it always seeks to establish interdependence between hitherto independent data; and it is a better theory if it does not sacrifice unity for diversity or diversity for unity. In this respect, science is like art: in both fields, greatness is the result of the most perfect reconciliation of "opposites": unity and variety, parsimony and adequacy.

The very structure of science is a kind of organized "community" of facts: it is a form that is more inclusive without being less harmonious, a rich variety brought to a focus. This method of contextualistic interpretation always involves reference to the perceptions and judgments of others. Science is the coordination of facts, and the very meaning of a fact is that it can meet the test of *social* verification. The distinguishing mark of scientific theory, moreover, is its public character, the result of a process of abstraction, generalization, and collective verification; because no belief has scientific validity so long as it remains private, the esoteric object of a single individual's perspective. It must be transmitted and interpreted to others and substantiated by them: it must be verified by stubborn and irreducible facts, admitted to be such by all qualified observers. It must, moreover, be consistent with established laws and theories, which in turn have been verified by scientists living and dead.

Because of the social nature of scientific method, every scientist must submit his personal observations and conclusions to the scientific community. For example, Professor Charles S. Minot, a distinguished anatomist of the last generation, concluded a series of lectures with these words:

> I do not wish to close without a few words of warning explanation. For the views which I have presented before you in this series of lectures, I personally am chiefly responsible. Science consists in the discoveries made by individuals, afterwards confirmed and correlated by others, so that they lose their personal character. You ought to know that the interpretations which I have offered you are still largely in the personal stage. Whether my colleagues will think that the body of conceptions which I have presented are fully justified or not, I cannot venture to say.[7]

This statement is the mark of a scientific man.

Therefore science, like common sense, is essentially social

---

[7] Quoted by Josiah Royce, *The Problem of Christianity* (1913; reprint ed., Chicago: University of Chicago Press, 1968), 2:225.

Science and World Community

in method: the difference being that science involves a much more elaborate correlation and comparison of social perceptions and judgments: a collective historic process knitting together many generations of all races and nationalities. The members of the scientific community are nurtured in a common tradition of thought: they are joined together not by force or herd-mindedness but by a common interest: the capacity of each for original thought and invention is a source of enrichment to all. These are the marks of a very high type of community. Such unity-in-diversity, transcending the barriers of race, nation, and class, is the very prototype of the ideal community: the worldwide voluntary fellowship of mankind.

The specialized and analytical character of most contemporary science, however, tends to counteract the communalizing and integrating effect of scientific method. So prodigious has become the accumulation of scientific data and research that it requires innumerable digests, abstracts, indexes, bibliographies, and bibliographies of bibliographies merely to keep some record of the ever-increasing mass of specialized research. Since life is too short to master more than a tiny fraction of this material, each scientist is inclined toward an ever-narrower specialization. Learning "more and more about less and less," he at last reaches the rather pitiful state of being unable to communicate with, or understand, his close professional colleagues. His "research" is understood by only a few initiates and is abracadabra to all other scientists, not to mention the general public. Digging away in his narrow vein, he may penetrate ever deeper into the mine of knowledge but he never comes up to the surface, to the point of vantage for a general survey. If not all scientists are to be characterized in these terms, at least far too many can be so described.

In consequence, the fast accumulating mass of information remains an uncoordinated aggregate, a chaos of "facts" rather than a unified body of culture. The layman, even more than the scientist, finds that the universe of knowledge has broken apart into a chaotic multiverse. In books, magazines, newspapers, and radio broadcasts he receives innumerable scraps of information about the nature of the world in which he lives; but the very multiplicity of facts that crowd in upon him serves to confuse him the more. His knowledge, in consequence, is as superficial and uncoordinated as it is diversified. He can no longer simply fall back upon scripture and immemorial tradition: the problems that confront him are too new and complex thus to be resolved; the transition from an old world to a new has gone too far. Lacking the traditional anchorage and any fresh grasp of the inner coherence of reality, he is an easy convert to irrationalist and antisocial ideologies, such as anti-semitism. If we are to escape such intellectual and moral anarchy, we must somehow diffuse among both scientists and laymen an understanding of the ultimate and general frame of existence. Unless in thought we can master our world we shall not be able to control it. What is required, therefore, is a great work of synthesis and general education.

Maintaining that scientists must create "an orderly world mind" to supplant the present "world dementia," H. G. Wells has suggested various devices to facilitate this task of synthesis. He has reemphasized the importance of an international language, such as Esperanto or basic English, which, like Latin in the Middle Ages, would serve as a basis for the free international exchange of ideas. He has proposed a world encyclopedia, not a mere mass of unrelated articles arranged in the specious order of the alphabet but a coherent expression of the spirit and best insight of the age. He has also suggested a great world institute, which would prepare digests and syntheses based upon research and thinking everywhere and which would systematically serve as the "world's memory." Such an institute would employ the most modern methods for the recording and dissemination of information, as for example microphotography, which enables the contents of a large library to be condensed in a small box and inexpensively to be reproduced in various parts of the world.

Such proposals could prove extremely valuable, but less mechanical and more fundamental is a profound intellectual reorientation: "a unified approach to knowledge and life." The conception of knowledge as an organic unity, "a system consisting of parts, related to one another, and interpretative of one another and the unity of the whole," must penetrate all the levels of science and education.[8] As a distinguished English physicist, J. D. Bernal, remarks, specialization has been carried so far that there is

> an enormous lag in the appreciation of the relevance of one field of science to another. For instance, chemists for a quarter of a century have failed to recognize that advances in physics and crystallography require not merely the revision but the complete recasting of the fundamental structure of their science, nor have the mathematicians appreciated the extraordinarily rich fields offered to them in the recent studies of the development of organisms. One effect of this is to hold back science just at those very places where its advance is most needed: the regions between recognized sciences.[9]

Already the interpenetration of the sciences, however, is being more fully recognized, as for example in recent biochemistry, biophysics, psychosomatic medicine, social geography, and broad humanistic studies such as cultural history. In consequence of this increasing appreciation of the unity of knowledge, a considerable number of educational institutions are abandoning the chaotic "elective system," whereby bewildered students encounter a haphazard succession of isolated "subjects," and are substituting an integrated curriculum.

Although such cross-fertilization of the sciences and integration of educational courses are extremely valuable, they must ultimately depend upon a comprehensive and dynamic synthesis. A detailed synthesis, as contrasted with the brief sketch which I have included in the present article, is very difficult to achieve. If we are to have a reliable "world view," the known universe must be "our oyster." We must intellectually possess it; we must understand it entire. To achieve this grasp is the task of a Titan, beyond the compass of any living

---

[8] Cf. Lewis Mumford, *The Unified Approach to Knowledge and Life* (Palo Alto: Stanford University Press, 1941).

[9] J. D. Bernal, *The Social Function of Science* (1939; reprint ed., Philadelphia: Richard West, 1980), pp. 114–15.

man. Aristotle in ancient Greece or Aquinas in the Middle Ages could sum up the total view, but the world as then understood was far more simple and synoptic. We must now rely not upon a single greater interpreter but upon a community of interpreters. We must no more give up the search for unity of thought than did men in ancient times but we must realize that the task now devolves upon an organized band of truth seekers, supplementing and complementing and qualifying one another's vision.

Many scientists have cried out with alarm against the proposal that they work together in an organized way, as in large measure they did during World War II. These protests are parallel to the many attacks upon planning in the economic and political sphere. They are based upon the false premise that freedom is inconsistent with organization. The fact that this premise is false we can see from many ordinary activities, such as a public dance, a baseball game, or an orchestral concert—from any cooperative activity in which order and individual expression are reconciled.

There is danger, of course, that men of thought will be tragically constricted by the forms of social organization: certainly this has occurred to a terrifying degree in certain parts of the world. The remedy is not intellectual anarchy because it brings the very tyranny to which we object: the real remedy is the interpenetration of so-called opposites, the achievement of free organization and organized freedom; not the buckling of minds to a preordained plan, but the creation of a plan by the free interaction of minds; in short, the attainment of a *free* community of interpretation. Such a community will not be achieved and preserved unless it is an integral objective of the plan. As Karl Mannheim has pointed out, freedom in a planned society means freedom actually provided within the plan—the provision of mediums for the free expression and interaction of minds and for the democratic "planning" of the planners—the guarantee that the community of interpretation will be free and democratic because it rests upon a community of persuasion. The task is not easy, but upon it depends the hope of the human race.

I began with a note of pessimism. I end with a note of optimism. It seems unlikely that mankind could achieve the magnificent structure of science and yet could so wantonly misdirect it as to destroy the human race. The grandeur of the achievement is an earnest of its proper use. Yet salvation does not come easily, and the burden is laid upon us all.

Chapter 4

The Artist as Outsider

Under the title, "The Plight of the Artist," this essay, somewhat abbreviated, was delivered as the Katherine Gilbert Memorial Lecture at Duke University, 23 October 1956. In its present expanded form, it was published in the Journal of Aesthetics and Art Criticism *16(1958). Some passages were incorporated into* Art and Human Values *(New York: Prentice-Hall, 1976), written in collaboration with Bertram Jessup.*

I. THE ALIENATED ARTIST AS A PRODUCT OF WESTERN CULTURE

Colin Wilson's *Outsider*, which has been widely read on both sides of the Atlantic, deals with the type of man that feels estranged from the world and his own deeper self.[1] One reviewer speaks of Wilson's theme as highly original. Actually, it is the old theme of "alienation" which Hegel expounded murkily in *The Phenomenology of the Spirit* and which the existentialists and many others have subsequently discussed.

Most of the examples of Outsiders cited by Wilson are artists or literary figures. Among poets or novelists he mentions Wells, Shaw, Tolstoy, Dostoevsky, Blake, Sartre, Camus, Hemingway, and T. S. Eliot, finding illustrations of alienation either in the lives of these authors or in their works. Among

[1] London and Boston, 1956.

nonliterary artists he speaks of Nijinsky and van Gogh. The philosophers whom he cites, such as Kierkegaard, Nietzsche, and Hulme, are half-poets. His examples would suggest that the problem of spiritual estrangement is, in large measure, artistic. Yet he treats his theme as if it were solely religious, and as if mysticism were the cure-all. This is to belie the full scope of the problem, which concerns the totality of our culture. I shall use his convenient term "the Outsider," but otherwise not refer to his book.

Paul Klee, himself a painter, had a more adequate grasp of the problem. He compared the artist to the trunk of a tree, and the work of art to the crown: "From the root the sap flows to the artist, flows through him, flows to his eye. . . . He does nothing other than gather and pass on what comes to him from the depths. He neither serves nor rules—he transmits. His position is humble. And the beauty at the crown is not his own. He is merely a channel." The tragedy of the modern artist, Klee maintains, is that the sap does not flow sufficiently from human roots—the participative life of the community. Artists suffer from social disunity—they are cut off from the larger spiritual whole. "We have found parts, but not the whole! We still lack the ultimate power, for the people are not with us."[2] The tragedy of which Klee speaks is exhibited in his own works: they are exquisite, subtle, ingenious—but they belong, in their intense and wayward subjectivity, to a private universe, and thus contribute to the very schizoid tendencies that he deplores. This is not the plight of a single painter or of a few artists only—it is much more pervasive. There seems to be a profound maladjustment between the creative life and the existing social order.

My contention is not that artists are necessarily Outsiders, or that Outsiders are necessarily artists. The artistically dumb and inarticulate person, such as Willy Loman in Arthur Miller's *Death of a Salesman,* suffers the worst pangs of alienation. As a means of spiritual communication, art breaks down

---

[2] *On Modern Art* (1948; reprint ed., London: Faber and Faber, 1966), pp. 13–14, 55.

the barriers between man and man, and thus provides a defense against estrangement. Many an artist *would* be an Outsider if he were not an artist. In our technological Western civilization, the artist *tends* to be an Outsider, but is not necessarily so.

He was less likely to be an Outsider in various other cultures. In medieval Europe, for example, art was an organic part of the community. The artist was a responsible workman expressing the collective values and traditions of his society. His art was essentially work well done—work that needed doing because it fulfilled the needs and expressed the emotions of his fellow men. Social collaboration was emphasized more than originality and freedom. A collective style, the Gothic, stamped every work of art, from a cathedral to a page of illuminated manuscript. Generations of artists, working without the overall design of a single master brain, could achieve the majestic and wonderful harmony of the great cathedrals because they labored to express a common faith and a common life.

In this respect, the medieval artist was reflecting the genius and essence of his civilization. The most striking sociological fact about the Middle Ages was the predominance of the intimate social group. The national state was weak or nonexistent; but the more close and primary association, such as the village or monastery, was the very focus of life. The ordinary man was primarily a member of a church, family, manor, or guild. The principle of group association was the basis of almost all activity, and not least in the arts.

Beginning with the Italian Renaissance and the rise of capitalism, the artist became much more of an individualist. This change coincided with the gradual breakup of the communal institutions of the Middle Ages and the rise of a competitive social order. Precapitalist medieval society was based upon the primacy of the spiritual, and thus art, which itself belongs to the category of spiritual values, had there a recognized function. But when the rising commercial civilization made acquisitiveness its dominant principle, the artist began to feel separate and detached. There was as little place for him in the coal mine or factory as at the Board of Trade. Consequently, he wanted some way to rationalize his cultural function and to protect the integrity of his art. So he became even more of an individualist than the business man, conceiving himself as a being apart and his art as exclusively an end-in-itself.

The change can be detected in Cellini's *Autobiography* and in Vasari's descriptions of his fellow-artists in sixteenth-century Italy. Cellini, in his unbridled individualism, was a harbinger of the modern age. The artists depicted by Vasari, although less mercurial than Cellini, were nevertheless set apart from ordinary people by their genius and their artistic vocation. They had cut their connections with the craftsmen's guilds and had become independent and self-conscious artists. The change, however, was gradual: not until the individualistic nature of Western civilization became firmly established, particularly during the Romantic period of the nineteenth century, did the idea become general that the artist is bohemian by nature—an eccentric and impractical dreamer, perhaps a genius, but certainly not a normal, well-adjusted member of society. If he chose external marks of nonconformity—for example, peculiarities of attire, such as the cape, the beret, the windsor tie; or residence in an artists' quarter, such as Montmartre, Grub Street, or Greenwich Village; or unconventionalities of behavior, such as keeping a mistress—these were the superficial signs of an inward detachment and estrangement.

Some artists have suffered deeply from this change. One thinks of Shelley's self-portrait in *Adonais*:

> A phantom among men, companionless . . .
> A herd-abandoned deer struck by the hunter's dart.

Or one recalls Vincent van Gogh, with his loneliness and hunger for community, which drove him first to a kind of Christian communism, then, with unabated religious ardor, to painting of feverish intensity, and finally to madness and suicide. Although suffering less extremely, many other artists have felt at odds with their society. The manifestoes of such schools as the Futurists, the Dadaists, and the Surrealists, express a feeling of opposition and estrangement.

II. THE BRONTOSAURUS PRINCIPLE

This historical change in the theory and practice of art has been the aesthetic counterpart of economic and social individualism. Within the last five or six decades, however, a gradual, silent, profound revolution has been taking place—a revolution in ideas, in techniques, in institutions that is carrying our social order from an individualistic way of life to a collective one. This revolution consists primarily in an increase in the number, variety, and scope of organizations. Vast, bureaucratized collectives, such as the business corporation, national farm organization, labor union, professional association, political party, military establishment, and governmental department are bulking ever larger in the lives of more and more people. Most titanic of all, the nation-state has become increasingly massive, complex, hierarchical, and multifarious. Even the "intimate" groups, such as the church, school, and fraternal order, have grown bigger, more impersonal and bureaucratic. In the evolution of social life, we have entered the Age of Dinosaurs.

It may be instructive to take this metaphor seriously and to glance at the history of the Mesozoic era. This was the age when the dinosaurs dominated all the land surfaces of the globe, and then rather suddenly disappeared. Although the causes of their disappearance are obscure, the ultimate disadvantages of huge scale appear to have outweighed the advantages. The dinosaurs evidently proved too ponderous and inflexible to cope with their environment. Perhaps the tremendous organizations of the twentieth century will meet with a similar fate. Some totalitarian states have already proved to be vulnerable. Professor Kenneth Boulding, in *The Organizational Revolution* (New York: Harper, 1953), coins the phrase, "the brontosaurus principle," to label the disadvantages of immense size. Up to a point, there are "increasing returns to scale," but "decreasing returns" in time may predominate. Huge organizations have a power and striking force that puny organizations lack. If it were not for such increasing returns, big government, big business, and big labor would not have evolved to their present brontosaurian proportions. But disadvantages are great. The struggle of giants may be very bloody, and the defense of each (as in the hydrogen bomb armaments race) may contribute to the insecurity of all. The principal disadvantage is the depersonalization and externalization of life. Only small groups can be personal. Members of a massive organization are essentially strangers to one another; the tie that binds them must therefore be impersonal and abstract, such as the fear of the police, or routinized propaganda, or stereotyped administrative techniques, or considerations of financial advantage. As the organization grows larger, its hierarchical structure becomes more elaborate, communication between the various grades becomes difficult, and the managers tend increasingly to regard the rank-and-file as mere pawns to manipulate.

The effect of the organizational revolution on human personality has been dealt with at length by such writers as David Riesman, Erich Fromm, and William H. Whyte, Jr. In the language of Riesman, the "inner-directed" type of person, whose motivation is provided by his own staunch values and convictions, is being supplanted by the "outer-directed" type, whose mirror-personality has no depth, who merely reflects what is going on around him, who is all things to all people, and who devotes so much attention to "selling" himself that he has no real self to sell.[3] Fromm similarly points out that in large collectivities "people are not able and cannot afford to be concerned with what is unique and 'peculiar' in each other." What matters is not what people *are* but how they *seem*. Hence they become so intent upon playing roles that their inner life dries up.[4] Whyte sees the consequences in the

[3] *The Lonely Crowd* (New Haven, 1950).
[4] *Man for Himself* (1947; reprint ed., New York: Fawcett, 1978), p. 74.

exaltation of collective mediocrity, the fear of being different, the unwillingness to "stick one's neck out."[5] All three writers present their argument with vigor and intelligence, and with a mass of telling evidence. They are confirming the fears that Alexis de Tocqueville and John Stuart Mill expressed so eloquently over one hundred years ago.

Whatever touch of exaggeration there may be in these interpretations, there is enough truth to explain much of the aversion of the creative artist. Art, in its very essence, is opposed to the deindividualizing and depersonalization of the new collectivism. The more an object has character and distinction in itself, the more it possesses an intrinsic value of its own, the more it stands out as incomparable and freshly expressive, the more likely it is to fascinate the artist. He seeks to snatch from the common dust whatever has a peculiar luster of its own. This is the reason that he tends to recoil from a world increasingly dominated by large, impersonal organizations, where people become faceless numbers.

Art thrives upon individuality, but individuality is not the same as individualism. By "individualism" I mean the system of every man for himself and devil take the hindmost. True individuality is violated by such a system. It also suffers when individuals are pressed into huge anonymous collectivities. Neither the older individualism nor the newer collectivism can be a substitute for genuine community—the real meeting between man and man.

III. THE GREAT SCHISM

One of the principal causes of the artist's alienation we have yet to mention. I shall call this "the Great Schism." In the early Middle Ages, there was a schism that divided the Eastern and Western Church, and in the fourteenth century there was another great schism in the Roman Church. We suffer from an even greater schism, and it affects the whole of our civilization.

Let me cite the illustration of the University of Washington

[5] *The Organization Man* (New York: Simon and Schuster, 1956).

where I teach. We often refer to the "Upper Campus" and the "Lower Campus." The Upper Campus is the scene of the arts, humanities, and social sciences. The Lower Campus houses the physical sciences and technologies. By and large, we on the Upper Campus do not understand or even talk with the people on the Lower Campus, and they do not understand or talk with us. What is true of the University of Washington is also true, in considerable measure, of every university in the Western world, and of the larger sphere of human affairs. Whether on or off the campus, the arts and humanities are not integrated with the physical sciences and technologies. This split is the Great Schism of modern civilization.

Its effect upon the arts is exemplified by our University buildings. By far the best architecture is on the Lower Campus. The structures that house the arts and humanities are imitative, eclectic, and often, in an overly-decorative way, ugly. They are not well-conceived, not functional, not really creative. The humanities and arts are fettered by traditions and controls which do not express what is vital in modern life. They are afflicted by a disease entitled "culture," one symptom of which is pseudo-Gothic architecture. The sciences and technologies, being relatively free from this disease, are able to find a much truer, more direct, more functional expression of their values. The effect can be seen in the relatively clean lines of the architecture on the Lower Campus.* The impressive new buildings at the Massachusetts Institute of Technology stand in similar contrast to the fussy and imitative architecture at most liberal arts colleges. There are notable exceptions, but the trend is incontestable.

It is a good omen that technology can thus find a fitting architectural expression. A new and beautiful kind of architecture has been discovered in cement, glass, steel, aluminum, and plastics, in techniques such as cantilever construction, and in the distinctive functions of our scientific age. The good architect works in close harmony with the scientist,

---

* Relationships between Upper and Lower Campus at the University of Washington are closer today than they were in 1956, and there is less contrast in the architecture (Author's note, 1981).

The Right to Hope

the engineer, the industrial designer, the town planner. Such builders as Le Corbusier, Neutra, Wright, and Gropius strive to heal the Great Schism. But, in most areas, the schism remains—a great gaping wound in the spiritual body of modern life.

The ordinary assumption is that industry, technology, and natural science have only a functional or intellectual import, with few value-implications, and that consequently the pursuits of the "humanist"—such as the cultivation of moral refinement and aesthetic discrimination—are quite separate and detached from scientific and industrial activities. The arts and humanities have been exiled to a realm of their own, more or less insulated from the main moving forces in our scientific and technological civilization. Science and invention make steady advances, but in the now detached realm of values and feelings, there is vacillation and uncertainty.

Can we expect art and morals to keep abreast of science? The basic goals of morality, such as love, wisdom, peace, and justice, were enunciated long ago by Lao-tsu, Buddha, Isaiah, and Socrates. The artistic masterpieces of ancient India, China, Egypt, and Greece have never been surpassed. "Progress" in these spheres seems difficult to define or gauge. But a society can become more rich and mature artistically, or enlightened morally; and it can either progress or retrogress in the *implementation* of its values. To articulate and apply the very complex morality suitable to a technological civilization, or to foster art and the creative life in a highly mechanized environment, is not easy. When civilization lags in these respects, we can truly speak of "retardation" in morals or art.

The Great Schism is largely a product of such uncoordinated and disparate levels of cultural development; and the alienation of the artist is a reflection within the individual of the resulting schizoid tendencies in the culture.

IV. The Effects upon the Artist

Art, being the sphere of creativity, personality, spontaneity, has suffered greatly from the mechanical rationalization of an industrial age. Insofar as the arts have flourished and have become truly popular, they have tended to become mechanized. They supply us with substitutes for creative experience—with amusement in place of real art, with passive response to mechanical stimuli instead of active personal participation and the joy of craftsmanship. The Mass Culture of today, unlike the folk art of the past, is concocted to make the cash registers jingle. Hired technicians exploit popular tastes, however vulgar, so long as it "pays." If sexiness, for example, "sells" well enough, it will glut the channels of mass-communication. The serious noncommercial artist, who refuses to compromise with market demand, finds himself in a precarious economic status. My main point, however, is not that the artist earns too little or that the public is indifferent to his work. An artist who wins acclaim and lives in comfort may still be an Outsider. The problem of spiritual estrangement is much more extensive than the question of popularity or compensation: it is the problem of achieving spiritual health in a depersonalized and mechanistic environment.

Contemporary artists have frequently expressed the tragic paradox of man's self-alienation in a mechanized world of his own making. This theme is embodied in the sculpture of Rudolf Belling: strange, semi-abstract, machinelike forms, half-human and half-mechanical. It is expressed in the paintings of Giorgio de Chirico or Fernand Léger: organic forms transposed into inorganic shapes and relations—the human and the nonhuman confounded. In music we find it in Arthur Honegger's *Pacific 231*, depicting the crude, raucous, overwhelming power embodied in a great locomotive; or in Paul Dukas' rendition of the old fable of the *Sorcerer's Apprentice*, symbolizing the tendency of tools and machinery to run wild and amuck. We detect the same theme in the early poems of T. S. Eliot, in which "hollow men, stuffed men" are buffeted about in the "waste land" of industrial civilization. We discover it in Karel Capek's *R.U.R.*, Aldous Huxley's *Brave New World*, and George Orwell's *1984*—satirical fantasies in which men are debased to the level of machines and machines take on life and dominate human beings. We perceive it in Franz

Kafka's strange fables, which represent the Ruling Powers as incomprehensible and heartless bureaucracies; and in Albert Camus's novel, *The Stranger*, which depicts an unwitting "murderer" who has lost sympathetic contact with other human beings and is dealt with by the authorities without pity or understanding. In a more comic vein, Charlie Chaplin has portrayed the pathetic little tramp trying to survive in a world much too large, too complicated, and too indifferent, and James Thurber has protested, in both drawing and story, against a confoundedly mechanized environment.

T. E. Hulme, Wilhelm Worringer, and José Ortega y Gasset have maintained that a fundamental motive of modern art is to break its vital aspect, to dehumanize it because of a deep disgust with "the human, all too human." According to these critics, the abstract, static, geometrical patterns of many paintings and statues represent a turning away from the mobile, organic, curvilinear lines of the human body, including the humanistic values that it symbolizes. Such art is more akin to the mechanical than to the human. One wonders whether it is subconsciously motivated by the artist's feeling of alienation from his fellow-man, or, less obviously, by an aversion to the machine. If the latter, the artist (in the words of Blake) is "giving a form to the devil so that he may be cast out."

One wonders also if the obscurity and complexity of so much modern art is a sign of the artist's alienation from his public. Max Eastman has denounced "the cult of unintelligibility," which he regards as the result, in large measure, of the failure to establish communication and sympathetic relations between the writer and his reading public. Similarly, the eminent musicologist, Hans T. David, has mentioned "the frightening chasm" that separates the contemporary composer and his audience. He points out "that our concerts are overwhelmingly devoted to music not of our age, and that our audiences have in their musical taste hardly reached the beginning of the century that is already half spent."[6] One again recalls the

---

[6] "The Cultural Functions of Music," *Journal of the History of Ideas* 12 (June 1951): 437.

lament of Paul Klee: "*Uns trägt kein Volk*—The people do not support us." The difficulty of so much modern art is partly a reflection of the complex and indecipherable character of the age, and partly a result of the absence since the Rococo period of any widely understood and well-established collective style. But it also results from too little sympathy and understanding between the artist and the public. This lack of rapport has marked effects upon the artist. Instead of thinking of his isolation as a misfortune, he may think of it as a virtue. He may try to free his art from all "extraneous" elements, to shun exhortation, conviction, representation, perhaps even meaning. He may endeavor to separate himself from tradition: to be different, independent, original, an individualist and innovator in his art. This anti-traditionalism is expressed in a bewildering succession of art movements, such as symbolism, post-impressionism, cubism, futurism, vorticism, imagism, expressionism, constructivism, dadaism, surrealism, and existentialism. There is a tendency to embrace each new movement because it offers the opportunity to be untraditional and to drop the movement as soon as it becomes a tradition. There is also an undercurrent of outright social rebellion. Unconsciously some artists have been trying to accomplish "the revolution by night," the revolution in men's dreams, while the masses accomplish "the revolution by day." We live in a revolutionary age, and the restless experimentalism in the arts is one phase of this revolution.

V. Freedom and Originality

In the course of this rebellion, the artist has attained a kind of freedom. All taboos are off: any style, any subject-matter is now permissible. Herbert Read declares: "It is a considerable achievement . . . of modern art to have made the world . . . tolerant (intellectually, if not politically) of variety. Modern art has broken through the artificial boundaries and limitations which we owe to a biased view of the human personality. . . . There is not one type of art to which all types of men should conform, but as many types of art as there are types of men."[7] Read considers it a great gain that the arts in nontotalitarian countries have been freed for almost unlimited experimentation.

There is much to justify his opinion; art has gained not only in versatility but in subjective depth and refinement. But the gain may not be as great as it appears. Perhaps the straining after originality is not so much a spontaneous act of freedom as a symptom of restlessness. Contemporary artists—particularly the avant-garde—are ill at ease in our mechanically rationalized civilization. They note the tendency toward the standardization of opinion, behavior, and production; and, as artists, they hate such regimentation. They realize that art, to be *real* art, must be original, and hence is necessarily opposed to conformity.

So far, the reaction is healthy. But there is a good deal of misunderstanding about the nature of originality. Contemporary artists too often suppose that it consists of atypicality— being *different*. They overlook the fact that the subnormal may be as atypical as the supernormal; madness may be as deviant as genius; disorder may be as "new" as order; atypicality may become repressively typical. This is not to deny that there have been sound reasons for much of the distortion, abstraction, and experimentation that has characterized modern art. Every age must solve its artistic problems in its own way; and it would be foolish to complain that artists do not paint or compose as their grandfathers did. There is much less justification for the social pressure, almost the compulsion, to conform to avant-garde standards.

Pointing out how difficult it is for the contemporary painter to defy "the canon of advancedness," Wyndham Lewis cites the remark of a painter friend: "It is strange, but we have to struggle just as hard today to do something . . . well, like painting a recognizable portrait . . . as formerly we had for years to struggle to be allowed to do something 'extremist' or whatever you like to call it. Today it is just the same thing the

---

[7] *Education Through Art* (1945; reprint ed., New York: Pantheon, 1974), p. 28.

other way around. One's dealer raises his eyebrows, frowns upon a more or less straight portrait when one sends it in. It has become like a religious orthodoxy."[8] One need not agree with Lewis' rather intemperate denunciation of "extremist" art, of which he was once a practitioner, to realize that the artist's "freedom" is not as absolute as it appears.

Our complex urban society has become differentiated into distinct groups, but within each of these groups there tends to be conformity to the group norms. The artist can enjoy the illusion of being autonomous—since he is deviant from the standards of "the Babbitts," "the Middle Class," "the Philistines," "the Unsophisticates"—while actually subservient to the standards of his own group. Paradoxically, this is true even when one's group, as in the case of the avant-garde, demands that the artist be original. This very demand makes it difficult for the artist to be so. Out of fear of being unoriginal, he hesitates to learn from an earlier tradition, an established artist, or even from his own earlier performances. Too often the effort of the artist is not so much directed at mastering a difficult craft or imbibing strength from the great traditions of the past as at catering to the taste preferences of sophisticates, under the illusion that to do so is to be original.

Originality is not easy to attain. Like happiness, it is elusive when directly pursued. The way to attain it is thoroughly to master one's craft and establish deep roots in one's culture. Even the greatest "innovators" return to the rich traditions of the past: one thinks of Walt Whitman, recapturing the majestic cadences of the King James Bible, or Yeats, hearkening to the lore and pristine lyricism of ancient Ireland, or Cézanne, reverting to the solid forms and rational order of Poussin's painting, or Bartók, drawing upon the folk melodies of his people. Even Picasso, that most audacious of inventors, is indebted to the classical figures of Greek art, the abstract patterns of Byzantium, the distortions of negroid sculpture, and the geometrical forms of Cézanne's landscapes. A work of art may be highly original even when the subject-matter is thor-

[8] *The Demon of Progress in the Arts* (London, 1954), p. 40.

oughly traditional. Innumerable Pietàs were painted or carved before Michelangelo took up his chisel, yet his *Pietà* is wonderfully fresh and original. What is important is the depth and intensity, rather than the novelty, of the experiences out of which art flows.

Genuine originality springs into being when the environment is ripe, when hand and heart correspond, when the mind is richly stocked with images, and when there has been hard preparatory work and a long period of creative brooding. Wang Li, an ancient Chinese painter, remarked: "Till I knew the shape of the Hua Mountain, how could I paint a picture of it? But after I had visited it and drawn it from nature, the 'idea' was still immature. Subsequently I brooded upon it in the quiet of my house, on my walks abroad, in bed and at meals, at concerts, in intervals of conversation and literary composition. One day when I was resting I heard drums and flutes passing the door. I leapt up like a madman and cried, 'I have got it!' Then I tore up my old sketches and painted it again. This time my only guide was Hua Mountain itself."[9] When there appears to be effortless creation, the hand has already been disciplined and the subconscious mind has already been peopled by bright images or floating melodies. Left to itself the mind is a desert.

VI. WHAT OF THE FUTURE?

The great question now is: Can community be regained, and if so, will true artistic freedom then become possible? I should like to consider two possible answers—one rather pessimistic and the other more optimistic.

The first view is that the contemporary artist *has* to alienate himself to keep his artistic integrity. The distinguished poet and critic, John Crowe Ransom, in a personal letter, quoted by permission, declares: "In all the arts as I imagine, but most certainly in poetry, and fiction too, the artist is lost because

[9] Quoted by Arthur Waley, *An Introduction to the Study of Chinese Painting* (1923; reprint ed., AMS Press, n.d.), p. 245.

there is no limit, no finitude, in the range of possibilities which suggest themselves to him. We know too much. And the scrupulous artist will not forego the exhibit of his own knowledge, which simply means being himself. Therefore he is lost in his own plenitude. And the good artists alienate themselves in so doing from the general public. I have seen this a thousand times." In support of Mr. Ransom's thesis, one might cite the eloquent argument of André Malraux.[10] Modern techniques of communication and reproduction, he points out, have showered us with an immense profusion and variety of artworks from every age and clime. This is true not only for the visual arts, with which Malraux deals, but for literature and even music. The artist is now aware of an almost infinite range of possibilities in styles, modes, and types of art, and this fullness of knowledge has become so much a part of his mind that he cannot divest himself of it. The art of all the ages being at his disposal, he does not depend for primary stimulation upon his immediate environment: art can feed upon art. He could still try to find a common idiom and seek a popular audience. But, for the reasons that we have already sketched, he feels pretty much an Outsider; so he is content to thread his way through the maze of artistic culture, vast, intricate, and sufficient unto itself. He may believe that only very complex art—too difficult for the masses—is adequate to depict the extreme complexities of modern life. "Is this state of advancement not fatal?" Mr. Ransom goes on to ask. "That is to say, is it not time for the new arts to originate from people with much less complex knowledge? I begin to think that the fullness of knowledge will still reside in the academy, and will not disappear, but that the arts will begin to come more and more out of the folk, which would mean that to some extent a new period in the arts must start from scratch. This is not comfortable to think about, altogether. But it has begun to enter into discussion, and it engages my own mind."

Another point of view—one which I hold—is that mankind, split into the élite and the masses, should be harmonized and

[10] *The Psychology of Art: Museum Without Walls* (New York, 1949).

made whole. The problem is to achieve a culture high in point of attainment yet broad in terms of participation—to achieve the wide sharing of excellence.

There are some moons that we should not cry for—the ones forever beyond our reach. If excellence is bound to be rare, we should give up the hope of its wide diffusion. But many of us are deeply loath to forsake the ideal of a *high* democratic culture as expressed, for example, by Walt Whitman in *Democratic Vistas*. The social foundation for a great American culture, he maintains, is both individuality and fraternity. "The all-varied, all-permitting, all-free theorem of individuality" must be combined with "another half"—"the personal . . . attachment of man to man"—to constitute a viable whole.[11]

We must not underestimate the difficulty of the task. To end the alienation of the artist, to bring art back to the center of life's text, to achieve an artistic culture high in its thrust and wide in its spread, to unite vivid individualities against the background of community—this is surely not easy. In a world increasingly dominated by very large organizations, we must seek out and cultivate the freer and more intimate groups. People must turn more and more for satisfaction to their membership in small, intimate circles, and these circles must become the focus of rich and immediate cultural activities. This program calls not only for a reappraisal of the values of community but for a reinterpretation of the cultural function of art.

Art is a matchless instrument for cultivating the sense of community. It breaks down the spiritual walls between human beings, while enhancing their individuality and free creativeness. All nonartistic modes of communication fail to portray adequately the inner man—his desires, hopes, misgivings, his joys and sorrows. These subjective states, in their uniqueness and inaccessibility, constitute the most private part of a man's being—they are not open to inspection and are least amenable to scientific description. The inmost core of personality would remain hidden and incommunicable if it

---

[11] *Leaves of Grass and Selected Prose*, ed. John Kouwenhoven (New York: Modern Library, 1950), pp. 477, 495, 505.

were not for art. But in a painting, drama, or musical composition, the duality of subject and object disappears.

The moods expressed in art are not separate from their objective mode of expression. The *what* of art is not separable from the *how*. When James Joyce, for example, expresses a shaver's disgust at "the clammy slather of the lather in which the brush was stuck," it is a clammy-slathery disgust that he is expressing. When Picasso expresses serenity with the muted colors and voluminous form of his *Woman in White*, it is a color-muted and voluminous serenity that is being expressed. The sadness of music is a peculiarly musical sadness: it is impossible, for instance, to give an adequate verbal phrasing to the majestic sadness of Chopin's *Sonata in B Flat Minor*. Even in poetry, the values cannot be formulated in any other words but that of the poem itself. There is a real creative synthesis, a fusion of mood with sensory configuration. As sensation blends with sensation to create a new quality (for instance, when notes combine to form a chord), so feeling or desire blends with sensation to create the aesthetic effect.

To depict the artist as necessarily a kind of spiritual Robinson Crusoe, forever marooned within the island of his own subjectivity, is to forget that the work of art is objective and yet is dyed with emotion and sensibility. The great artist, moreover, transcends his merely private feelings; he explores and creates by means of his art the values of mankind. In this sense, he is never *wholly* an Outsider. We must therefore repudiate the extreme individualistic and isolationist theory of art that we have inherited from the nineteenth century. We cannot agree with Whistler when he wrote in his "Ten O'Clock Lecture" (1888): "The master stands in no relation to the moment at which he occurs—a monument of isolation—hinting at sadness—having no part in the progress of his fellow men." We can no more agree with recent critics, such as Clive Bell, when they write in a similar vein.

Art should neither be debased to a merely utilitarian role nor separated from the main business of humanity. We should live as whole men, not with our muscles or brains alone, but with our eyes, our ears, our entire mind and body, with the full range of our creative capacities. Thus to live we must respond to the world in a skilled, active, artistic way, our senses aroused, our tastes cultivated, our imaginations at work. Art, as Ruskin and Morris maintained, must lend its grace to the most familiar objects and scenes: daily attire, common utensils, homes and gardens, streets and neighborhoods, places of work and play. Artists must join with engineers, city planners, and civic-minded leaders in bringing a new decentralization, cleanliness, order, and comeliness into our urban environment. The artistic phase must enter much more pervasively into industry—with less emphasis upon mere volume of productivity and more emphasis upon fine workmanship and good design. A revival of creation, in the form of various amateur pursuits, has already begun, and it must be energetically promoted by schools, discussion groups, neighborhood art centers, and all sorts of music and art circles. We must limit the mass-standardization so characteristic of the coca-cola-and-television dimension of our civilization. The emphasis should be upon personal creativity and *active* participation in small, friendly, face-to-face groups, such as choirs, bands, orchestras, dramatic and dance circles, and art-center workshops. The main basis of living for the artist, as for the ordinary citizen, should be neither isolated individualism nor anonymous collectivity, but the meeting between man and man, each giving and responding from a center of inwardness.

These changes cannot be achieved apart from the planned development of free communities—in a cultural not merely a political, sense. We must have a real working faith in community, in the values of personal interdependence, cooperation, collaboration, and sharing; and these values must be cultivated by morals, religion, technology, science, art, and town planning. There must be a general renewal and decentralization of our culture, putting humanity before machines, and considerations of welfare ahead of profit. What is required is not a revival of medievalism, which had its own grievous faults, but a new synthesis that will put personal relations at the focus of life while utilizing, selectively, the immense creative potentialities of a technological and scientific age.

In the past, human associations have been determined chiefly by economic necessity, geographic proximity, and blood ties. In the practicable future, technology will free men from bread-and-butter cares and supply them with leisure, easy communication, and rapid transit. They will then flock together upon the basis of friendship and mutual interests— scientific, artistic, recreational, etc. A new kind of decentralization, functional rather than merely geographic, will thus be achieved. The Great Schism between science and humanism will be terminated, and the artist will regain the sense of community.

Chapter 5

Community in Time of Stress

An address delivered at the University of Colorado in celebration of the Centennial of John Dewey's birth (1859). Published in the University of Colorado Studies. Series in Philosophy 2 *(August 1961). Some passages were woven into* Ethics and the Human Community *(New York: Holt, Rinehart and Winston, 1964).*

I

To some of the jaded minds of the twentieth century, John Dewey appears curiously old-fashioned. He seems to belong to a time long ago when men were intensely excited by the potentialities of science and technology. Standing as on a mountain top, the older prophets of science pointed to a land of promise that stretched as far as they could see. Men like Bruno, da Vinci, Campanella, and Bacon were enthralled by the boundless prospect of scientific and technological progress. Descartes, for example, believed that mankind would eventually understand "the force and the action of fire, water, air, the stars, heavens, and all other bodies that environ us," and would thus become "the masters and possessors of nature."[1] Condorcet predicted that "the human race, freed from its chains, removed from the empire of chance," would

[1] *Discourse on Method*, Part 6.

advance "with a firm and sure step on the pathway of truth, of virtue, and of happiness."[2]

This vision recurs in the works of John Dewey. His philosophy is a sustained advocacy of the scientific method in every possible field of inquiry.

> In spite . . . of all the record of the past [he has declared], the great scientific revolution is still to come. It will ensue when men collectively and cooperatively organize their knowledge for application to achieve and make secure social values; when they systematically use scientific procedures for the control of human relationships and the direction of the social effects of our vast technological machinery. Great as have been the social changes of the last century, they are not to be compared with those which will emerge when our faith in scientific method is made manifest in social works.[3]

It is sad to turn from such vigorous affirmation to the views of many recent thinkers. Ironically, it has been within the last few generations, when science and technology have been achieving their greatest triumphs, that the most pessimistic ideas have been expressed. At the beginning of this century, Henry Adams declared that "we are like monkeys monkeying with a loaded shell," and that "science is to wreck us."[4] Even William James, although not given to dour predictions, warned that modern scientific man may be like the child drowning in a bathtub because he has turned on the water without knowing how to turn it off. More dogmatic in his predictions, Oswald Spengler declared that "optimism is cowardice"; the West is doomed; our machines have got out of hand and are dragging us to the precipice. Although H. G. Wells began his career as an inveterate optimist, he predicted in his final book the clean extinction of the human race. "There is no way out or round or through," he announced. "It is the end."[5]

[2] *Progres de l'Esprit Humain*, Epoque I.
[3] *Philosophy and Civilization* (New York, 1931), pp. 329–30.
[4] *The Selected Letters of Henry Adams* (New York, 1931), p. 237.
[5] *Mind at the End of Its Tether* (London: Didier, 1945), pp. 4, 15.

The Right to Hope

John Dewey turned away from such unmitigated pessimism and revived the heady idealism of the first great prophets of science and technology. Nevertheless, he was deeply moved by the troubles as well as the hopes of civilized man. He was intensely aware that the swift development of science had precipitated our confusions and catastrophes. As late as October 1948, he wrote that "the crisis in which man is now involved all over the world, in all aspects of his life," had its origin "in the work done by physical inquirers in the relatively aloof and remote technical workshops known as laboratories." But he also noted that "the attack upon science as the responsible and guilty party is terribly one-sided in its emphasis."[6] It neglects the many and great human benefits that have accrued from science, and it fails to understand the main cause of the modern crisis.

That cause, declares Dewey, is the incongruity between new things and old. Science works within an institutional framework developed in prescientific days. To cite but a single example, the human race has been threatened with atomic annihilation because the ancient institution of war is a very present anachronism. We shall not escape danger and confusion so long as our marvellous new powers are fettered and perverted by preexistent institutional conditions.

The main trouble, Dewey avers, is that the scientific revolution has not been extended to the human sphere. The swift development of *physical* science and technology has not been balanced by a comparable advance in the *human* sciences and skills. We are technically far more competent than any previous generation, but we are socially incompetent. As a consequence, physical power has increased very rapidly, social harmony has improved very little. The supreme need—the very mandate of human survival—is the cultivation of better human relations.

This we cannot achieve if we delimit science and fence off a humanistic sphere. The schism between science and human-

[6] *Reconstruction in Philosophy* (enlarged ed., 1948; reprint ed., New York: Beacon Press, 1957), pp. xxi, xxiii.

[80]

ism, which is the worst disease of our civilization, must be terminated if we are to rectify the glaring disparity between advanced *physical* and retarded *human* knowledge. "A vision of a day in which the natural sciences and the technologies that flow from them are used as servants of a humane life constitutes the imagination that is relevant to our own time. A humanism that flees from science as an enemy denies the means by which a liberal humanism might become a reality."[7]

Dewey admits most of the facts alleged by the critics and detractors of our machine-civilization. "Quantification, mechanization and standardization," he declares, "have invaded mind and character, and subdued the soul to their own dye."[8] But the disintegration of individuality is not due to science or technology per se—it is due to the failure to reconstruct our ideals and institutions so as to meet the realities of the new age.

There is nothing final or fatal about the present state of society. We can, in great measure, learn to foresee the possible consequences of existing conditions, and can take sides in favor of the consequences that are to be preferred. If we develop the capacity to think scientifically about human relations and social issues and to employ the fecund means of physical and social technology in behalf of a significantly human life, we can create a new and richer individualism—not opposed but integral to community. This is Dewey's answer to the pessimistic views of a Spengler or a Henry Adams.

In his later books, such as *A Common Faith* and *Art as Experience*, Dewey puts less exclusive emphasis upon the method of scientific intelligence and more emphasis upon the values of feeling, impulse, and imagination. He seeks a larger balance and integration of all fields of human culture: science, technology, art, religion, morality, and social action. The principal need is to tap our intelligence and imagination to the fullest in developing a whole and balanced civilization. But Dewey never abandoned his early confidence that a scientific

[7] *Individualism Old and New* (New York, 1930), pp. 155–56.
[8] Ibid., p. 24.

humanism can be used greatly to enhance individuality and enrich the common life.

II

Technology and science operate within an institutional context; their potentialities for good or ill depend largely upon this setting; they must be guided and controlled if their constructive development is greatly to outweigh and exceed their destructive tendency. What, then, can guarantee their right use?

As an inveterate democrat, Dewey rejected the ideal of a governing oligarchy of scientists and technicians. He believed in the fullest communication and interaction between the experts and the people. The experts should educate the people to enlarge their political choices by revealing the new alternatives that science and technology make possible, but the people, in turn, should educate the experts to make clear the wants of the community and thus to clarify the great ends that scientific intelligence should serve. "A class of experts," Dewey points out, "is inevitably so removed from common interests as to become a class with private interests and private knowledge, which in social matters is not knowledge at all." "In the degree in which they become a specialized class, they are shut off from knowledge of the needs which they are supposed to serve." [9] What is required, therefore, is not a governing élite but a vigorous democracy that brings the people and the experts together in close and fruitful communication.

If scientific experts acting *alone* should not be trusted with power, neither should any other limited group. We must not permit technology and science—which can either destroy civilization or give it a new birth of freedom—to fall under the control of a grasping plutocracy, or a scheming military cabal, or an irresponsible political crew, or a small administrative bureaucracy. The only safe and right control, Dewey tells us

[9] *Public and Its Problems* (1927; New York: Swallow Press, 1954), pp. 206–7.

emphatically, is that exercised by an educated and democratic community, operating through its responsible leaders and representative agencies. "For every sphere of life that fails in its democracy," he declares, "limits the contacts, the exchanges, the communications, the interactions by which experience is steadied while it is enlarged and enriched." [10]

His ideal of a democratic community is opposed to both oldstyle individualism and newstyle collectivism. Let us briefly consider what he finds objectionable in each of these alternatives.

In common with many thinkers, he has pointed out the limitations of the traditional individualistic creed. It is not that freedom or individualism is a false value, but that men have pursued a false freedom and individuality. The philosophers of individualism have tended to think of each man as an island unto himself, and freedom as merely the "right" of the individual to be left to his own devices. Hobbes, Bentham, and even Locke have defined the self in terms of self-concern, and have conceived freedom as immunity from institutional restraints. The underlying assumption of many individualistic books is made explicit in Rousseau's early writings: man is born free and equal, but he has become enslaved in a network of social relations; freedom will be regained by striking off the repressive bonds of society. This point of view assumes that the individual exists in separate abstractness, antecedent to society and complete within himself. But the self is not some kind of abstract monstrosity squatting outside of the world of interaction and change. It is being perpetually wrought out— it is being created and recreated under the influence of associated life.

The only way to achieve a decent measure of individuality, to attain real, effective, operational freedom, is to develop sympathetic relations with other things and especially other people. This is not to deny the contention of John Stuart Mill that the independent and original person enriches society far

[10] "Creative Democracy—The Task Before Us," *The Philosopher of the Common Man* (New York, 1940), p. 228.

more than the tame conformist, and that a very important kind of freedom is the right to make one's own decisions. Dewey's attack upon the conformist is one of the main themes of his philosophy. But, as he also persistently maintains, it is utterly unrealistic to frame a theory of freedom or individuality that takes little account of the myriad social ties that bind every man to his fellows. The conception of individuality as an antecedent and ready-made thing is a fiction propagated long ago by the rebels against feudal collectivism, but it is now preserved and repeated by those who oppose the remaking of society. As Dewey remarks: "The ultimate refuge of the stand-patter in every field, education, religion, politics, industrial and domestic life, has been the notion of an alleged fixed structure of mind." [11] It is theoretically false and practically insupportable to maintain that an individual can realize his potentialities merely by being left alone. Negative freedom— the right to be left to one's own devices—should be subordi-nated to positive freedom—the presence of all those resources and opportunities necessary for growth and self-realization. "Freedom from restriction," declares Dewey, "is to be prized only as a means to a freedom which is power; power to frame purposes, to judge wisely, to evaluate desires by the conse-quences which will result from acting upon them; power to select and order means to carry chosen ends into operation." [12] One of the principal errors of traditional individualistic liber-alism, as Dewey has frequently pointed out, is to conceive freedom much too narrowly and negatively.

Dewey's denial of oldstyle individualism is no more explicit than his rejection of newstyle collectivism. Long before such writers as David Riesman and William H. Whyte, Jr., had de-nounced "the organization man," Dewey had attacked the mass-hypnosis of propaganda and commercial advertising, the manipulation of human behavior by "public relations experts"

[11] "The Need for Social Psychology," *Psychological Review* 14 (July 1917):273.
[12] *Experience and Education* (1938; reprint ed., New York: Macmillan, 1963), p. 74.

and "political machines," and the mental treadmill of the overgrown bureaucracy, whether it be a governmental agency or a private corporation. He realized as keenly as anyone that the depersonalization of life is not only a threat but a constant reality in a society dominated by massive organizations. He was one of the first to expose the totalitarian mentality, whether fascist or soviet, but he recognized that the organizational revolution, with its deadening and desensitizing of all things personal, is a main force even in America. It seemed to him unlikely that such antihuman tendencies would long prevail. They would reduce the world to a cemetery, or there would be a change of direction.

He not only denounced the practices of collectivism but refuted its philosophical fallacies. Just as the oldstyle individualists thought of the self as a preexistent and ready-made entity, so the newstyle collectivists have conceived the superorganization, whether private or public, as a fixed entity and an end-in-itself. But an organization is not a *substance*, it is not a *thing*—it is a *process* and an *achievement*. Any vital organization is a way of interacting and associating so "that experiences, ideas, emotions, values are transmitted and made common."

> To this active process [declares Dewey], both the individual and the institutionally organized may truly be said to be subordinate. The individual is subordinate because except in and through communication of experience from and to others, he remains dumb, merely sentient, a brute animal. Only in associating with fellows does he become a conscious center of experience. Organization . . . is also subordinate because it becomes static, rigid, institutionalized whenever it is not employed to facilitate and enrich the contacts of human beings with one another.[13]

Individualism is on the wane, and there appears to be no prospect of a revival in its old form. Collectivism is waxing—but here and there appear signs of slackening and decay. The

---

[13] *Reconstruction in Philosophy* (New York: Beacon Press, 1957), p. 207.

"realists" who see no other future for mankind than the accentuation of a dehumanizing collectivism are blind to these signs and have too little faith in the inner resistance and resilience of mankind. Neither the social homelessness of individualism nor the mass anonymity of collectivism can supply any deep and lasting happiness. The false dilemma, "individualism or collectivism," no longer appears so inescapable; and the choice that it presents no longer appears attractive. Dewey realized that neither horn can provide the genuine freedom and realization that each promises, and that there is a *third* alternative that avoids the extremes and distortions of the other two. "The essential human reality is neither one of individual nor of collective existence," as Martin Buber has written, "but lies in the relation between man and man, and is a matter between me and you."[14] This alternative I shall call "community," and the remainder of this essay will be devoted to an explication of it. Modern civilization is desperately in need of reorientation, and this fresh orientation should be around the concept of the human community. In Dewey we find a profound and eloquent spokesman of this concept.

III

If we are to use *community* as a basis for human renewal, we must employ the term in a broad and fundamental sense. Any narrow meaning cannot serve as an instrument for that new endeavor of critical examination, creative synthesis, and social reconstruction through which alone our civilization can survive and advance. The meaning, at the same time, should not be vague and sentimental. In the writings of Dewey we can find the basis for a definition of community that is as precise as it is broad.

E. C. Lindeman, who has been strongly influenced by Dew-

---

[14] Foreword to E. A. Gutkind, *Community and Environment* (London, 1953), p. viii. Despite Buber's more religious orientation, there is a deep affinity between him and Dewey.

ey, distinguishes between a "functional" definition, which emphasizes psychological process, and a "structural" definition, which emphasizes geographical pattern. "A community," he declares in his functional definition, "is any process of social interaction which gives rise to a more intensive or more extensive attitude of interdependence, cooperation, collaboration, and unification." [15] This "functional" definition stands in contrast to a "structural" definition like that of Robert M. MacIver. The members of a community, declares MacIver, must not only engage in "the interactivities of common life" but must "occupy together a definite place on the earth's surface." [16]

Dewey's idea of community is more like that of Lindeman than like that of MacIver. It differs from Lindeman's definition, however, in its emphasis upon freedom as well as interdependence. Community, as Dewey uses the term, refers to all the ways and means by which human beings *freely* recognize and realize their interdependence. In a family, a neighborhood, a circle of friends, in a cooperative activity of any sort, in relations that are very intimate and in relations that are far-flung in time and space, men realize the fact of interdependence and mutuality. A community exists when this experience is made the *voluntary* basis of social coherence.

It must be admitted that Dewey sometimes speaks of "the community" so as to imply a geographical locale, but in many other passages the term is not so limited. The emphasis is upon participation and sharing rather than physical proximity. "Associated or joint activity is a condition of the creation of a community," he points out. "But association itself is physical and organic; while communal life is moral, that is emotionally, intellectually, consciously sustained." [17] It develops through the give-and-take of communication rather than through mere

[15] "Community," *Encyclopedia of the Social Sciences* (New York, 1930), 4:103.
[16] Robert M. MacIver and Charles H. Page, *Society* (New York, 1949), pp. 9–10, and MacIver, *Community* (1917; reprint ed., New York: Arno, n.d.), p. 107.
[17] *Public and Its Problems*, p. 387.

adjacency. In the past, human associations have been determined chiefly by geographic proximity; but technology is supplying the means of rapid transit and easy communication, and the leisure to enjoy them. Human beings are now flocking together upon the basis of friendship and mutual interest rather than accidental juxtaposition in space. New bonds, functional rather than geographic, can thus be forged, and the limitations of the immediate locale can be transcended. Dewey's emphasis upon community as a *process* fits the new age of freer communication and transit.

Communication that is truly communal is not the impersonal sort that so frequently prevails in modern life. Baker Brownell, who has reflected deeply upon the subject, employs the term *community* to denote "a group of people who know one another well." "It refers, not to the abstract relationships of men with men as functions or elements of a great society, but to the association of whole, concrete, living, breathing persons with each other." [18] Dewey shared Brownell's concern with the intimate pattern of living, and he agreed that community must have its roots in intimate personal relationships. But he was also greatly concerned with the problem of national and worldwide unification. If we are to discover a principle broad enough to pervade our culture and to promote world harmony, we cannot limit our key concept to the small, intimate group. Josiah Royce, in one of his less metaphysical essays,[19] proposed that the ideal of community be extended to include all mankind. He pleaded for a world order based upon a profound respect for the manifold loyalties and indigenous cultures of the earth's many peoples. Such a pluralistic world-order, the richer because of its diversity, is only a hope and an aspiration—but if it should ever be realized, it would deserve the name of "the Great Community." Dewey realized that we need both the *intensity* of community as insisted upon by

[18] *The College and the Community* (1952; reprint ed., New York: Greenwood Press, n.d.), pp. 43–44.
[19] *The Hope of the Great Community* (1916; reprint ed., New York: Arno Press, n.d.).

Brownell and the *extensity* of community as envisaged by Royce; and he addressed himself to the problem of reconciling the two.

"There is no substitute," he declared, "for the vitality and depth of close and direct intercourse and attachment." In "its deepest and richest sense a community must always be based upon the smaller intimate unions of human beings living in immediate contact with one another." [20] But the great problem of our age is not simply to rehabilitate the small community but to bring the entire family of man into relations of amity and interchange. Peoples that have been suddenly thrown into pointblank atomic range of one another *must* learn to live together as friends and neighbors. As Auden writes in one of his poems: "We must love one another or die."

The right solution, as Dewey points out, is to recognize the interdependence of the great and the small community. It would be vain to attempt a fundamental reconstruction of human life by operating *only* at the local level. Wise national and regional planning is imperative to the welfare of localities. Even the whole international order must be taken into account—for without peace, the development of every community is in question. Also the wide perspectives and the far-flung contacts of the great community will "flow back into local life, keeping it flexible, preventing the stagnancy which has attended stability in the past, and furnishing it with the elements of a variegated and many-hued experience." [21] On the other hand, we cannot create the great community unless we reconstitute and conserve the values of the intimate group—the love that comes only with intimacy, the appreciation of personality in its wholeness and integrity, the sense of mutuality and interdependence. As Dewey points out, there is little chance to cultivate regard for distant peoples "as long as there is no close neighborhood experience to bring with it insight and understanding of neighbors." [22]

[20] *Public and Its Problems*, pp. 211–13.
[21] Ibid., p. 216.
[22] Ibid., p. 213.

The future world-order may be either a collective or a community. A collective would be imposed from the top, regimenting the masses to an obedient conformity. One can imagine a bureaucracy swollen to planetary proportions, efficient in giving orders and manipulating minds, and equipped with the secret police and the centralized army to enforce its every decree. A world-community, on the other hand, would spring from the intimate cells of social life—the family, the neighborhood, the work group, the circle of friends, the cultural or civic association. It would thus be a community of communities, expressing in its very structure and institutions the cooperative habits of its constituent groups. Only human beings who have acquired the inner disposition of a life in common are fit citizens of the world. Hence they must not lose or forsake their distinct and local communities, in which they learn the ways of fellowship. The community of mankind will be the richer because it is differentiated and the stronger because it sinks its roots deep into the small communities. No one has realized this fact more keenly than Dewey.

In his early writing, there is less emphasis upon the values of diversity. For example in *Democracy and Education*, the stress is rather upon communication and like-mindedness:

> There is more than a verbal tie between the words common, community, and communication. Men live in a community by virtue of the things which they have in common. What they must have in common in order to form a community or society are aims, beliefs, aspirations, knowledge,—a common understanding—like-mindedness as the sociologists say. . . . The communication which insures participation in a common understanding is one which secures similar emotional and intellectual dispositions—like ways of responding to expectations and requirements.[23]

In the books of his later years, Dewey continues to emphasize communication and common understanding, but there is a

---

[23] *Democracy and Education* (1916; reprint ed., New York: Free Press, 1966), p. 5.

new sharp emphasis upon the importance of variety. "To learn to be human," he declares, "is to develop through the give-and-take of communication an effective sense of being an *individually distinctive* member of a community."[24] (My italics.) Difference, he insists, is as important as likeness—there must be a spiritual kinship yet a rich diversity. His intense reaction against fascist and communist regimentation had much to do with this change in emphasis.

A community, as distinct from a totalitarian organization, is a unity of the multiform. Its members are raised up by and bound up in relations which stir in the depths of their being and constitute their very nature; but the closer the unity, the greater the individuality of its members. This is the case in any true fraternity; we treasure our friends the more because of their unique qualities. Concrete individuality is enhanced, not emasculated and repressed by fraternal bonds—each person steps forth in his singleness to join the other single ones in giving and receiving: he is neither isolated in the midst of humanity nor depersonalized in a social ant-heap. The members of a community are able to bridge their differences in virtue of the things they have in common, but they are able to enrich one another by the rich ferment of their contrasting individualities.

The mark of community is to be found in the quality and not the quantity of human associations. An indiscriminate passion to "belong" produces the condition which H. G. Wells, in his *New Machiavelli*, attributed to the "progressive" town of Bromstead—"a dull, useless boiling up of human activities, an immense clustering of futilities." Modern technology has already made our lives over-complicated. There is too much hustle and bustle; too much overcrowding of the surfaces; too rapid a sequence of impressions and events. Life should be less contested—it should be simpler and calmer and deeper—with fewer things to do and time to do them better. Excessive sociability merely adds to the din and confusion of life.

William H. Whyte, Jr., complains that the organization man

[24] *Public and Its Problems*, p. 154.

is "imprisoned in brotherhood," but it is not really brotherhood that is imprisoning him. The passion to dissolve oneself
in the group is not a sign of community but of the contrary. As
Dewey shrewdly remarks:

> We should not be so averse to solitude if we had, when we
> were alone, the companionship of communal thought built into
> our mental habits. In the absence of this communion, there is
> the need for reinforcement by external contact. Our sociability
> is largely an effort to find substitutes for that normal conscious-
> ness of connection and union that proceeds from being a sus-
> tained and sustaining member of a social whole.[25]

An indiscriminate togetherness, or lack of reserve, is a viola-
tion of community rather than an expression of it. To cherish
another person is not merely to enjoy his company but to
respect his privacy—to be sensitive to what is inviolably his
own.

This sensitivity implies recognition of the autonomy and
intrinsic preciousness of personality. All through Dewey's
educational and political philosophy runs the strong, unde-
viating protest against the manipulation of human beings,
whether by misguided educators or by advertizers, "public-
relations experts," "scientific managers," and "social engineers." We Americans, with our advanced technology, are
experts in our knowledge and manipulation of impersonal
forces; and we are tempted by that achievement to try to manipulate men with the same skill and ingenuity as we manipulate machines. But the manipulation of men, as Dewey often
insisted, is the destruction of community.

A community differs from an association in which some are
using others as mere tools. The relation is between *man and
man*, not between man and thing, or between man and person
regarded as thing. A human being may look at another and say
to himself: "You exist for my use." He then regards the other
as a mere "it," not as a subject like himself but as an object to
be manipulated. His attitude is different when he thinks:

---

[25] *Individualism Old and New*, pp. 87–88.

"You are a person like me, and each of us should be sensitive to the rights and claims of the other." The first attitude leads to domination, the second to fellowship. There is thus a radical distinction between the relation "I-you" and the relation "I-it." Not only does the "you" differ from the "it," but the "I" in the first relation differs fundamentally from the "I" in the second. The first "I" is a real person in a world of persons; the second "I" is a depersonalized individual in a world of things. A person is fully a person only in relation to other persons. He is not a real person so far as he regards others as things, as mere objects or implements. The communion between man and man comes about only when each regards the other as an end. This is not always possible—to live, we need to use things, and what is more to the point, to use human beings. But in a real community, the means-relation between individuals, the "I-it" relation, is subordinated to the ends-relation between persons, the "I-you" relation. Hence Dewey insists that "the supreme test of all political institutions and industrial arrangements shall be the contributions they make to the all-round growth of every member of society."[26]

A community, in fostering the freedom and growth of its members, differs from an involuntary association. Robert M. MacIver and Charles H. Page, in their book *Society*, suggest that even a prison is a community, since it is an "area of social living." This is quite contrary to Dewey's usage. There may, of course, be community-feelings among the inmates, but so far as the prison is an embodiment of force, it is the very opposite of a true community. Even if coercion be exercised by organizational pressure or "the force of circumstance" rather than by human beings with weapons, the element of free mutuality, and therefore of community, may be lacking. Community is the interaction of real, authentic persons, and to the extent that individuals are creatures of force, circumstance, or pressure, they lack the essential attribute of perso-

---

[26] *Reconstruction in Philosophy*, p. 186. The thought, as I have stated it in this paragraph, is similar to Martin Buber's *I and Thou*, but Dewey is arguing from more naturalistic premises.

nality. Here Dewey agrees with the existentialists. "So far as I choose, I am," declares Karl Jaspers. "If I am not, I do not choose." In the words of Jean-Paul Sartre, "I am my liberty."[27] Community, being an association of persons, requires the autonomy that is inseparable from genuine personality.

It has often been pointed out in criticism of the theory of "community" that it implies social conservatism and preservation of the status quo. This charge cannot be leveled against the concept as Dewey has interpreted it. The sterilization of social diversity and the standardization of thought and conduct are characteristic of collectivism rather than of genuine community. A community by its very nature is a union of free and various personalities. Like Socrates' love of Athens, the spirit of community is no mere acceptance of convention, no uncritical or credulous orthodoxy, no buckling under to force or prejudice—it involves courage, independence, free inquiry, and respect for individual rights.

To sum up, the term *community*, as Dewey employs it, refers to a process rather than to a locality. Although it is not limited to the small, intimate group, its roots are personal rather than abstract and impersonal. It is based upon free mutuality rather than mere like-mindedness. It consequently excludes any relation of dominance or exploitation. Far from being a settled and finished affair, it is perpetually in the making; and the individual's commitment to it is not simply retrospective but dynamic and progressive.

IV

Perhaps there never has been and never will be a full-fledged community, unalloyed by alien elements. In its perfection, it is an ideal and not a present fact. But it is a

[27] Karl Jaspers, *Philosophie* (1932; reprint ed., Chicago: University of Chicago Press, 1970) 2:182; and Jean-Paul Sartre, *L'Etre et le Néant* (Paris, 1949), p. 127. Cited by John Wild, *The Challenge of Existentialism* (1955; reprint ed., New York: Greenwood Press, 1979), p. 117.

Community in Time of Stress

legitimate ideal, and it is sometimes realized in considerable measure. Dewey, with his pragmatic bent, has emphasized the means to its realization. "Not all who say Ideals, Ideals, shall enter the kingdom of the ideal," he has declared, "but those who know and who respect the roads that conduct to the kingdom."[28]

With his great faith in the potentialities of a scientific civilization, he has contended that science and technology can be reoriented and directed toward the cultivation of intimate groups and free, cooperative personalities. Enough statistical evidence is already at hand to suggest that technology is, in fact, beginning to create a new type of social order—less centralized, less congested, less impersonal, and less bureaucratic: that the centripetal city is giving way to the centrifugal city and the small community. Under the influence of automobiles and other forms of rapid transit, suburban villages and outlying trading centers are multiplying, and some of the smaller towns are beginning to revive. There is a relatively new and quite marked tendency to build factories away from congested centers of population. In the United States, these new factories are springing up in little towns in the South and West and in other nonmetropolitan locales. Although the great cities are continuing to grow, the population increase in the suburban areas is much faster than in the city proper. There are many signs that the metropolis is in process of far-reaching transformation.

A very important factor in this movement toward decentralization is the development of new sources of power—electric and atomic. The inexpensive conductivity of electric power, and the small bulk of the material from which atomic energy is derived, reduce the difficulties in the distribution of fuel and therefore permit the location of power stations and factories in scattered areas near the consumers.* The first great steps have been taken to exploit a new source of fuel, deuterium (heavy

[28] "The Pragmatic Acquiescence," *New Republic* 49 (5 January 1927):189.
* I no longer regard the spread of suburbia and the exploitation of nuclear energy as desirable, but I have retained the wording of my address to preserve its original integrity (Author's note, 1981).

hydrogen), which is literally as plentiful as water and which would cost far less than any present source of power. The effect of such a scientific breakthrough can scarcely be exaggerated: it would make for a fundamental restructuralization of industry, and if properly guided, for a much more decentralized economic and social system.

In response to decentralist tendencies, there has sprung up a number of writers and thinkers: men like Arthur E. Morgan, David Lilienthal, Baker Brownell, Frank Lloyd Wright, Lewis Mumford, and Charles Perry. They believe that the new technological trends toward decentralization can be greatly stimulated by social planning and community organizing. They hope eventually to establish a person-centered culture and intimate group life upon the basis of the new technology and the rich resources of modern civilization. How rich these resources really are and how adaptable to a humane and uncluttered existence has been made wonderfully clear in Mumford's books, especially in his *Technics and Civilization* and *The Culture of Cities*. They establish, beyond peradventure of doubt, the realism of Dewey's faith in the wise uses of science and technology.

It will be necessary, however, to resist the tremendous pressure to use technology primarily for the benefit of big business, big government, and bigness of every sort. The events of this century, Dewey avers, have proved that private economic collectivism, with its massive concentration of both capital and labor, produces both anarchy and oppression. State socialism, far from being a satisfactory substitute, likewise leads to the triumph of "the organization man" and the suppression of individuality. As Dewey remarks: "Roughly speaking, the 'haves' stand for private collectivism, and the 'have nots' for state collectivism. The bitter struggle waged between them in the political arena conceals from recognition the fact that both favor some sort of collectivism and represent complementary aspects of the same total picture."[29]

---

[29] "What I Believe, Revised," in Gail Kennedy, *Pragmatism and American Culture* (Boston, 1950), p. 32. This essay originally appeared in Clifton Fadiman, ed., *Living Philosophies* (New York, 1939).

Dewey does not propose a return to the older philosophy of laissez faire. As I have pointed out, he is equally opposed to an atomistic individualism and a totalitarian collectivism. His ideal is the free meeting of man with man, doing equal justice to the two interpenetrative sides of human nature, the individual and the communal. He recognizes that governmental power, wisely employed, can itself be a mighty force in strengthening individual freedom and voluntary associations. "Political activity can, first and foremost, engage in aggressive maintenance of the civil liberties of free speech, free publication and intercommunication, and free assemblage."[30] In this period of hyperorganization, civil liberties become more necessary and precious than ever before. Second, government can throw its support to underprivileged groups, such as Negroes, slum-dwellers, and migrant agricultural workers. A government actively devoting itself to the protection of the weak and unfortunate can greatly increase the total freedom of its citizens even when it sternly curbs the unduly powerful. Third, the provision by government of better health, education, security, and cultural opportunities, and the right political control of science and technology, can immensely facilitate individual liberties and encourage voluntary associations. As Dewey declares, the principle of the free community "does not deter political activity from engaging in constructive measures. But it does lay down a criterion by which every political proposal shall be judged: Does it tend definitely in the direction of increase of voluntary free choice and activity on the part of individuals" and autonomous groups?[31]

Dewey thus rejected an exclusive emphasis upon the state and political activity as the means to communal living. The principle of "cooperative association" or "shared experience," rather than a mere political program, is the heart of his faith. He looked forward to the development of cooperative voluntary endeavor in innumerable fields—recreational, artistic, religious, scientific, technical, and economic. Any group en-

---

[30] Ibid., p. 33.
[31] Ibid., pp. 33–34.

gaged in socially useful activity may become aware of its functions and its responsibilities, and may seek to extend its services and to enrich and enhance its members. Dewey thought of a democratic government as largely the servant of such voluntary cooperative groups, with their many and diversified interests. "The state," he declares, "remains highly important—but its significance consists more and more in its power to foster and coordinate the activities of voluntary groupings."[32] Its function is mainly to integrate and augment the various techniques which free associations have at their disposal.

> I am not optimistic enough [Dewey declared] to believe that voluntary associations of individuals, which are even now building up within the cracks of a crumbling social order, will speedily reverse the tendency toward political collectivism. But I am confident that the ultimate way out of the present social dead end lies with the movement these associations are initiating. Individuals who have not lost faith in themselves and in other individuals will increasingly ally themselves with these groups.[33]

A true community, whether it be a voluntary association or a democratic government, seeks the mutual enrichment and enhancement of its members. This seeking may be exhibited in a number of ways. First, the community can intensify the ties between the persons that compose it—they can learn to know and appreciate one another; they can explore the methods of new and deeper and more delightful intimacies. Second, the community can achieve a richer differentiation—its members can become more free, more creative, more various, more genuinely individual, finding ways of adjusting, or even enjoying, their differences. Third, the community can cultivate its traditions and extend its temporal span—through memory, it can reach back into the past, and through expectation, it can reach forward into the future—it can thus become, in the

[32] *Reconstruction in Philosophy*, pp. 203–4.
[33] "What I Believe, Revised," p. 35.

words of Edmund Burke, "A partnership . . . between those
who are living, those who are dead, and those who are to be
born." [34] Fourth, the community can widen its spatial extent
and break through the limits of narrow parochialism—its
members can seek ways to transcend the barriers of nationality, race, class, and creed, and to establish the cultural basis of
a universal human community—not as a uniform, monolithic
organization but as a community of communities.

The crucial question for our age comes down to something
like this: Do we want to live merely as rootless, isolated, un-
attached individuals; or do we want to surrender our real personal selves to the brontosaurian jaws of collectivism; or, finally, do we wish to cultivate genuine communities within a
many-faceted and pluralistic society? *216110*

Since the death of John Dewey, liberalism has become
strangely timid. Attacks from the right and the left have un-
nerved and demoralized it. Philosophy, which should be giving strong and positive guidance, has turned almost exclusively to narrow and refined problems of analysis. Few philosophers, especially among the more fashionable, display any
interest or competence in social philosophy. The words of
Dewey echo from a different world of thought: "Better it is for
philosophy to err in active participation in the living struggles
and issues of its own age and time than to maintain an immune, monastic impeccability, without relevancy and bearing
in the generating ideas of its contemporary present." [35] I dare
to think that this conception of philosophy will revive. If so it
does, Dewey will once again serve America as a wise guide
and counselor, and his theory of community will help to in-
spire a renascent liberalism.

---

[34] *Reflections on the Revolution in France*, ed. Conor C. O'Brien (1910;
reprint ed., New York: Penguin Books, 1976), p. 93.
[35] *Essays Philosophical and Psychological in Honor of William James* (New
York, 1908), p. 80.

Chapter 6

Crisis and the Spirit
of Community

The Presidential Address delivered before the twenty-seventh annual meeting of the Pacific Division of the American Philosophical Association at Stanford University, December 1953. Published in the Proceedings and Addresses of the American Philosophical Association, Volume 27, *November 1954. In a modified version it formed the concluding chapter of* Ethics and the Human Community *(New York: Holt, Rinehart and Winston, 1964).*

I

There is no simple explanation of the crisis of our age. We used to blame the fascists for our ills, and then we blamed the communists; but Hitler and Stalin would never have had a chance if modern civilization had not been monstrously defective, and until the basic evils are removed, new spectres will arise, time and again, to haunt us.

We civilized human beings have been pouring new wine into old bottles. We have fathomed many of the secrets of the universe; we have invented the mechanical means to wipe out poverty and to build a world community; but we have attained no corresponding cultivation of feeling and no adequate spiritual assimilation of the new ideas and techniques. Our "progress" has been far more swift in the techniques of homicide than in the arts of peace.

For the last three or four centuries, the main impetus of Western civilization has been toward the hypertrophy of self-asserting drives and the corresponding decline of self-transcending impulses. The prevailing culture is competitive; economically the individual competes with others for livelihood; socially he competes for prestige. Value-standards are frequently based on rivalry and tend toward conflict. Individuals are often pressed into groups, but the groups tend to be pitted against one another and to be divided by barriers of class, nationality, race, religion, language, and custom. The resulting conflicts among individuals and groups are potentially so destructive that the survival of civilization is in question.

Modern dictatorships have sought to prevent social disintegration by extreme coercion, leader-worship, and chauvinism. But the cure is worse than the disease. The alternative to both a communist or fascist dictatorship and an individualistic system of devil-take-the-hindmost is the cultivation of free, cooperative communities. Indeed, the development of cooperative ways of living to replace the present competitive ways is the prime need of mankind at this critical juncture of history.

Such unity cannot be imposed from without: it must spring from within. It cannot be attained by the intimidation, imprisonment, or extermination of those who do not agree. As Plato pointed out in the eighth and ninth books of *The Republic*, some societies, like certain personalities, act and speak as if they are unified, but they are masking inner anarchy by a feverish outward assertion of unity, noisily proclaimed and coercively enforced. Such specious unification suppresses really vital elements of internal life. *Genuine* unity, which reconciles freedom with organization, can be achieved only by that complex of psychological factors which gives inner cohesion to a community. Institutions and material resources are necessary, but they are vacuous without a spiritual substance to give them force. A civilization based upon the growth of material power will break down, as modern civilization has been breaking down, unless there is a coherent core of values that unites its members.

These values must be more than a set of abstract moral precepts. Cerebrally a man may know his duty but unless his passion fights on the side of his intelligence, he may be wicked, foolish, or mechanical in his behavior. Not only understanding of the good, therefore, but *devotion* to it is required. Without this devotion, a person is very likely to think to himself, "Why should I bother about society?" His attitude will remain egocentric or his efforts will be half-hearted. But when he acquires a profound emotional conviction that his deals are based upon the nature of things, he may be lifted right out of his listless humdrum self and gain immensely in strength, forcefulness, and passion. Such transformation and integration of a whole life can be called, in the wide sense, "religious."

I use this word with some hesitation because of its supernaturalistic connotations. Like many philosophers, I count myself a naturalist. I regard the transition from myth to science—a transition still far from complete—as the grandest achievement of the human intellect. Most of what passes under the name of "religion" seems to me myth, archaic or decadent.

However, I do not feel that naturalistic philosophers are justified in their usual neglect of religion. As Whitehead has said: "In considering religion, we should not be obsessed by the idea of its necessary goodness. This is a dangerous delusion. The point to notice is its transcendent importance; and the fact of this importance is abundantly made evident by the appeal to history." [1] Even superstitious beliefs and practices, since they have taken such a deep hold upon human nature, reflect some genuine need. Although religion has carried over into civilization many of the crudities of barbaric imagination, its very persistence and universality indicate something fundamental, something that may perhaps be given a noble and

---

[1] *Religion in the Making* (1926; reprint ed., New York: New American Library), p. 18.

unsuperstitious expression. Moreover, in its more sophisticated expressions, religion is a far cry from primitive superstition. It is comforting to the antireligious to suppose that the deeply religious man is Homo ignorans or Homo stupidus rather than Homo sapiens, but this supposition is not justified. In thus asserting the value and importance of religion, I am not a revivalist—I have no desire to propagate any existing religion. Also, I have no wish to consider the arguments of natural theology. I should like to call your attention, however, to certain facts about religion that provide a clue to the interpretation of human needs. In this age of crisis we can no longer take any of the basic forms of culture for granted. Human beings must become transparent to themselves: they must understand the main forces and institutions that move them; and they must learn to control the deep irrational forces that when uncontrolled, drive men like autumn leaves in a storm. Only thus can they hope to find a vision deep and realistic enough to guide them safely in this age of monstrous tensions, and to make the arts of life prevail over the newfangled prodigious techniques of death. If, as some empiricists believe, religion is a passing phase of human culture to be superseded by an antimetaphysical and scientific mentality, it might still be necessary to find a "moral equivalent."

II

I shall start with a very curious fact. The cultural conditions that have given rise to so much great art, science, philosophy, and statesmanship have been singularly unproductive of original religious genius. We can recall scientists such as Archimedes, Newton, Pasteur, Darwin, and Einstein; or artists such as Praxiteles, Michelangelo, Shakespeare, Bach, and Cézanne; or philosophers such as Plato, Descartes, Spinoza, Hume, and Kant; or statesmen such as Pericles, Cromwell, Jefferson, Garibaldi, and Churchill. All these men flourished in relatively complex civilizations. Many of them lived in great cities or sophisticated centers of culture such as Athens and Florence.

We do not look to such cities, however, for the original founders of the world's religions. Not a single major religion has ever been initiated by any of the myriad human beings in our teeming metropolises or even in our more cultivated towns and villages. The truly commanding figures—men such as Lao-tsu, Confucius, Buddha, Zarathustra, Shankara, Jesus, and Mohammed, from whom have flowed the main religions of the world—belong to simpler societies of the dim and misty past. We can point to a few relatively minor cults and their founders, but how limited in comparison with the superlative religious geniuses and their world-conquering faiths! Of course, we have had our derivative figures, our preachers and theologians aplenty, but no great seminal religious minds. How shall we explain this paradox?

We cannot say that religion, like wine, must be old in order to excel. Certainly the immediate followers of Buddha, Jesus, or Mohammed took no such view. Age may add a certain taste and bouquet to religion but it cannot account for its original tang.

Neither can we say that religion is essentially primitive and therefore must disappear as civilizations mature. It has been too deeply felt, too pervasive and fundamental a factor in human culture, to be dismissed as belonging solely to humanity's nonage. It *originates* in less complex societies, but it proliferates and spreads over a vastly wider area. For example, Christianity sprang up in the villages of Judea, but it took the effete civilization of Rome by storm and has exerted a mighty role in the world ever after. Moreover, many highly cultivated human geniuses, such as Socrates, Bach, and Einstein, have been intensely religious. In this respect, religion is very different from magic, which usually remains local and primitive.

There must be some point of contrast between the ancient, simple, and naive communities and the relatively modern, complex, and sophisticated societies that will help to explain the fact that religion *arises* mainly in the former but *spreads* in the latter. The essential difference, I venture to think, is that the simple community is close, warm, intimate, and human whereas the complex society is relatively cold, abstract, and impersonal. In the simple community, men know one another very intimately as concrete, vivid, flesh-and-blood personalities within the family, neighborhood, or small circle of friends. In comparison, our modern societies function largely by way of abstract indirect relations such as communication by telephone, radio, printed page, or casual economic transaction.

The difference between these two types of human associations can be made clearer by exaggeration. The following quotation from Karl R. Popper's book, *The Open Society and Its Enemies*, is apropos:

> We could conceive of a society in which men practically never meet face to face—in which all business is conducted by individuals in isolation who communicate by typed letters or by telegrams, and who go about in closed motor cars. (Artificial insemination would allow even propagation without a personal element.) Such a fictitious society might be called a "completely abstract or depersonalized society." Now the interesting point is that our modern society resembles in many of its aspects such a completely abstract society. Although we do not always drive alone in closed motor cars (but meet face to face thousands of men walking past us in the street) the upshot is very nearly the same as if we did—we do not establish as a rule any personal relation with our fellow pedestrians. Similarly, membership in a trade union may not mean more than the possession of a membership card and the payment of a contribution to an unknown secretary. There are many people living in a modern society who have no, or extremely few, intimate personal contacts, who live in anonymity and isolation, and consequently in unhappiness.[2]

This contrast between the concrete and abstract society is our clue for the interpretation of religion as a cultural force. In the intimate community, human beings first learned the ways of fellowship. Only within the matrix of loving personal rela-

---

[2] *The Open Society and Its Enemies* (1950; 5th rev. ed., Princeton: Princeton University Press, 1966), p. 170.

tions, men like Jesus and Buddha and Lao-tsu came to spiritual birth. Here they developed the capacity for personal communion, which is, I believe, the main psychological source of religion. Here men of genius created the great religious symbols and myths of the human race, whereas in our abstract, sophisticated, kaleidoscopic societies, where even "charity" is institutionalized and thereby depersonalized, the geniuses are relatively untouched and uninspired by the close communion of persons. They can perhaps create great art, science, philosophy, and statecraft but cannot create great religious symbols.

A city such as ancient Athens was intermediate between the concrete community and the depersonalized society. Its citizens developed some of the mobility, intellectual detachment, and blasé individualistic attitudes characteristic of modern urbanites, but without altogether losing the closeness and intimacy of the primitive blood-brotherhood. Their dramatists, such as Aeschylus and Sophocles, and their philosophers, such as Socrates and Plato, were still religiously loyal to the community—the sacred city-state. In reading philosophical works such as the *Apology* or plays such as *Oedipus the King*, we feel the conflict and tension between the old ideal of clan-fellowship and the new dawning ideal of free "emancipated" individuality. The communal religious spirit was still creatively at work among the Greeks, but it was not so intense as among the less sophisticated people of Judea. In comparison, the mobile, restless, uprooted denizens of our gigantic modern cities are much farther removed from the spiritual milieu in which the world's great religions have originated.

Yet the hunger for communion persists even in the most contactless societies. Love is too instinctive ever to be wholly repressed. However depersonalized our human relations become, we try to reach across the abyss that separates man from man and man from the surrounding universe. Here, then, is the secret of religion's power. The basic impulse of the higher religions is to extend the community-mindedness of the close, intimate, concrete group to the wider sphere of the immense, impersonal, abstract society.

It is no accident, therefore, that religion uses the language of the face-to-face community: that it speaks of love, fellowship, brotherhood, communion, the fatherhood of God. It is no accident, also, that the higher religions seek to project these concepts to their widest possible scope. For this is the meaning of the higher religions: to take the love that is cultivated in the most intimate circles and to extend it to the widest circles that the human imagination can trace.

Primitive religions similarly have expressed the values of the intimate tribal community, but they have failed to project these values beyond their original parochial limits. Lacking catholicity, they have remained local and often temporary. Likewise the more parochial religions of civilized peoples, such as Japanese Shintoism, have lacked the power to spread. In contrast, the greater contagiousness and viability of the higher religions are the result of two factors: first, they have expressed the primordial values of the intimate community and thus have tapped the deepest roots of human feeling; and second, they have sought to extend these values to the widest compass and thus to universalize them.

III

If religion is rooted in community, this fact must be reflected in its fundamental nature, and indeed this is exactly what we find. A religion such as Hinayana Buddhism can exist without the worship of God; and a profoundly religious man, such as Spinoza, can forego any belief in the supernatural; but no religion and no religious individual, I am inclined to think, can exist without the realization, in some form, of the values of community.

Admittedly there are many definitions of religion and these vary widely. Leo Tolstoy, James Leuba, and others have listed definitions by the score. However, most authorities in the field—such as Emile Durkheim, R. R. Marrett, Rudolf Otto, and John Macmurray—seem to be agreed that the psychological essence of religion is the feeling of sacredness, or as some would prefer to say, of holiness. As Principal John Oman has declared: "If we are to have one mark of religion, it could only be this sacred . . . valuation. . . . Everything that is sacred is in the sphere of religion, and everything in the sphere of religion is sacred."[3] The attitude of sacredness is a complex sentiment—something of a blend of wonder, awe, gratitude, and tender admiration.

In his masterful work, *Primitive Religion*, Robert H. Lowie maintains that the feeling of sacredness is evoked primarily by abnormal stimuli—the mysterious, weird, extraordinary, or supernatural. To a philosophic mind, however, even the most common objects can be sensed as wonderful and strange. What could be more mysterious, for example, than the universe of Hume, in which one incomprehensible event follows with incomprehensible regularity after another incomprehensible event! However, one must be something of a mystic or a poet to feel, as Walt Whitman did, the sacred and unutterable mystery of the most common things, such as leaves of grass.

While admitting Lowie's contention that the sense of astonishment is at the heart of religion, I believe that more is involved in religious experience than blank wonder and awe. There is also the feeling that what is deep and mysterious within oneself is akin to what is deep and mysterious in the object. "What is that," St. Augustine asks, "which gleams through me and smites my heart without wounding it? I am both a-shudder and a-glow. A-shudder, in so far as I am unlike it, a-glow in so far as I am like it."[4] The unlikeness lends to religious experience its note of dread, but the likeness lends the note of tender exaltation. This sense of kinship seems to me not the whole of religion but an essential part of it. Toward sacred objects we generally feel a fundamental bond of community.

[3] *The Natural and the Supernatural* (1931; reprint ed., New York: Arno Press, 1972), p. 69.
[4] *Confessions*, Book 11:9.

The need for communion and self-transcendence springs largely from man's primordial solitariness. In the little span between birth and death, each of us experiences the poignant fact of being confined within his own skin and limited by his isolated individual selfhood. Each of us is curbed and hemmed in by the massive restrictive force of human culture, its laws, its taboos, its conventions. Each tends to feel small and insignificant and powerless before the vast indifference and immensity of nature. Especially in moments of crisis, every man, like a shipwrecked Robinson Crusoe, wants to escape from the little island of his own selfhood. Religion is the return from solitariness to community—it is man's endeavor, by an inward personal adjustment, to make himself at home in the world. By cultivating the religious sense of community, he escapes from his loneliness and self-alienation.

The form of this self-transcendence is not necessarily attachment to a *human* community. In the religion of the Crow Indians, for example, the essential quest is to attain, in solitary vigils, communion with a supernatural Guardian Spirit. Likewise the higher religions have their recluses, each seeking a lonely understanding with his God. Even in the case of the mystic, however, the value of religious withdrawal is never to be found in *mere* isolation but in the spiritual union of the self with the nonself: "the flight of the alone to the alone." To this extent all religion is social.

To say that religion is social is not to deny the value of solitude. Withdrawal, such as that of Mohammed into the desert or Jesus into the Garden, is characteristic of deeply religious personalities. The most intense religious experience requires inward concentration and mental detachment. Moreover, the need for privacy as a counterweight to the raucous mechanization and crowd pressure of modern life has never been greater than at present. If withdrawal is not a mere perversion, however, it is eventually followed by a return, with the recluse's contribution to society enriched by the clarification of intention and the concentration of power achieved in solitude. Individuality and sociality in religion are not exclusive and ought reciprocally to enrich one another. Religion has long affirmed the paradox that modern psychiatry has re-discovered—that one realizes oneself by transcending one-self.

To sum up, if sacredness is the subjective essence of religion, community is its appropriate object and characteristic expression. This community may be conceived as human or sublimation of the love and friendship experienced in the superhuman, natural or supernatural; but even where it is conceived by nonhuman terms, devotion to it is very largely a close, personal, face-to-face community. Hence all the great world religions have originated in simple, primary-group societies like that of ancient Palestine, where men most naturally learn the ways of intimate fellowship. Religion is both individual and social, but the individual fulfills his deepest spiritual longings not by parting himself off from the surrounding world, but by the attainment of a harmony of the self with the nonself.

IV

When I use the term *community* I have in mind a basic relationship which all of us have experienced innumerable times. It is a simple fact that human beings are interdependent—they are held together and unified by the attitude and practice of cooperation, collaboration, reciprocity, and sharing. *Community*, in this sense, refers to all the ways and means by which human beings *freely* recognize and realize their personal interdependence. It stands in contrast to the type of relation that exists when one person regards another as a mere tool; it involves a person-taken-as-person relation among free individuals, a relation of mutuality.

Such mutuality is exhibited in any close friendship. Friends do not want to be isolated from one another, nor to master or dominate one another. If they are *real* friends, they recognize the right of each to be *himself* and therefore to be different. Indeed, this is the mark of friendship, that neither regards the other as a tool, to use, to exploit, to over-rule—that each respects and loves the other for what he is, a free independent human being. Friendship is a unity in which variety is cherished, and hence is the form of spiritual integration which most fully protects the freedom of its members. It thus exhibits the free mutuality, or unity of individualities, which I call "community."

Religion, for the most part, is the consecration, generalization, and sublimation of the values of community. If we think of the small, intimate community as the microcosm, we can say that religion tends to interpret nature or supernature as the macrocosm. The microcosm is the community writ small, the macrocosm is the community writ large.

Similar generalization may occur in philosophy. For example, in the idealistic metaphysics of Josiah Royce, the concept of community takes on a cosmic sweep. "The history of the universe," he declares, "the whole order of time, is the history and order and the expression of this Universal Community."[5] Likewise Alfred North Whitehead has envisaged nature as a hierarchy of societies, the higher embracing innumerable lower ones. "The universe," he explains, "achieves its values by reason of its coordination into societies of societies, and into societies of societies of societies."[6] Within these societies, moreover, "the entities take account of one another. What happens is an emergence, a fusion of entities, a mutuality. . . . A structural togetherness is being realized."[7] Even the entire universe is conceived as an "interlocked community" of events.

Nevertheless, the metaphysics of Royce or Whitehead is a philosophy rather than a religion, because it is primarily intellectual. Someone has said that a sophisticated man's religion is his philosophy taken emotionally and practically. If so, the

---

[5] *The Problem of Christianity* (1913; reprint ed., Chicago: University of Chicago Press, 1968), 2:273.

[6] *Science and the Modern World* (1925; reprint ed., New York: Free Press, 1967), p. 145.

[7] From W. E. Hocking's summary of a conversation with Whitehead in Paul A. Schilpp, ed., *The Philosophy of Whitehead* (Evanston, Ill.: Northwestern University Press, 1941), p. 387.

philosophy must be fundamentally transformed and take on the character of a sacred vision and way of life. Religion and philosophy may spring from the same metaphysical need—the need for some final adjustment of the Self to the great Other— but they differ fundamentally in the way in which this need is expressed.

V

There have been many religious variants of the idea of community. The totemism of primitive religion, for example, springs from the deep communal feeling of the tribe. At this level, man is scarcely aware of his individuality; he conceives of himself as an indivisible part of the cycle of all human and natural forces. Even inorganic objects are conceived of as animate and as having intimate affiliations with the human community. Primitive tribesmen really believe what St. Francis of Assisi taught, that the birds and beasts and fishes are their "little brothers." The tribe, as they conceive it, includes animals as well as human beings. There are many other types of primitive religion besides totemism, but it is perhaps characteristic of all of them to express, in some generalized form, the values of the primitive community.

In recognizing the communal nature of such religions, we do not need to agree with the French anthropologist, Emile Durkheim, who maintains that primitive religion is the worship of society, the sib, clan, or tribe, in the guise of totemic or other supernatural symbols. On the contrary, we should recognize that the concept of community is imaginatively projected far beyond the bounds of human society. As Gilbert Murray has said, religion is frequently "the groping of a lonely-souled gregarious animal to find its herd or its herd leader in the great spaces behind the stars."[8]

In the more civilized religions, there have been many variants of the idea of community, such as the Confucian doctrine of universal kindness, the Buddhist emancipation from

---

[8] *The Stoic Philosophy* (London: George Allen and Unwin, 1921), p. 42.

selfhood, the Taoist sense of cooperation with nature, the Hindu vision of an all-embracing spirit, the Hebraic passion for social justice, the Christian fellowship of all men in God. Among the more universal religious creeds probably the most important is mysticism. W. T. Stace, in *Religion and the Modern World*, has maintained that all religion, either implicitly or explicitly, is mystical. Although this contention may be an exaggeration, mysticism is at least a very characteristic and fundamental expression of the religious impulse.

The basic doctrine of the mystic is that reality is an ineffable spiritual unity and that outer reality is identical with the essence of the human self. This creed is stated in the paradoxical words of Chuang-tzu, the ancient Chinese Taoist: "The universe and I came into being together; and I, and everything therein, are One."[9] The mystic believes that it is possible to know this unity directly and intuitively and that this knowledge is supremely good.

Some mystics contend that the One is an undifferentiated unity and that consequently all discriminations made by the human intellect are false. For example, William Wordsworth in an early manuscript fragment, described a stage in his mental development in which he regarded all forms, images, and ideas as "the very littleness of life" and as "relapses from the one interior life that lives in all things." It seemed to him that all our puny conceptual boundaries are manmade and that the true reality is a seamless unity:

> In which all beings live with god, themselves
> Are god, Existing in the mighty whole,
> As indistinguishable as the cloudless East
> At noon is from the cloudless west, when all
> The hemisphere is one cerulean blue.[10]

Such mysticism might be called "negative," because its object, however piercing, is empty and undifferentiated. There

[9] Robert O. Ballou, *The Portable World Bible* (1939; reprint ed., New York: Penguin Books, 1976), p. 508.
[10] *The Prelude*, ed. Ernest De Selincourt (London: Oxford University Press, n.d.), pp. 512–13.

are a good many examples of this type of mysticism in the history of religion. Its votaries teach the unreality of material things; they often regard the flesh and spirit as at war; they view the ordinary world as a prison or scene of exile; and they reject science as a basis of belief.

There is another type of mysticism that can be called "positive," which is illustrated by a later stage in Wordsworth's mental development. In his famous "Lines" composed near Tintern Abbey, he speaks of an intense and joyous mood in which "we . . . become a living soul" and "see into the life of things." In this passage describing a trancelike state, the one unitary "life" does not exclude "things" in the plural. There is no turning away from the copious variety of nature. Because of the mystic vision, nature seems more previous rather than less—and real at its own level. Consequently, Wordsworth is

> A lover of the meadows and the woods,
> And mountains, and of all that we behold
> From this green earth . . .

Whereas negative mysticism apparently sacrifices community to a featureless unity, positive mysticism retains the love of individualities which is the distinguishing mark of community. It realizes that the unity of love is higher than the unity of inclusion. Love enjoys the difference between "you" and "me" and hence it is the natural bond of community. Consequently, a positive mystic such as William Blake, in his religious poem *Jerusalem*, spontaneously employs the language of the intimate community:

> I am not a God afar off, I am a brother and friend:
> Within your bosoms I reside and you reside in me.

The unity is very close, but it is a unity of distinct persons. The *each* is not submerged in the *all*.

It may be that the difference between positive and negative mysticism is not so radical as it appears. All mystics emphasize the ineffable character of the mystical vision; and perhaps, as W. T. Stace has suggested, some mystics speak in negative terms because they feel that all positive characterizations are inadequate. Neither the positive or negative terms are to be taken literally because the truth of mysticism, they maintain, is incapable of conceptualization.

I should be inclined toward such a nonliteral interpretation not only of mysticism but of almost all religious creeds. The fantasies about the gods, about heaven and hell and grace, about Yahweh and Gilgamesh and Valhalla, are the poetic expression of the essential claim of religion—that community is sacred. If we look at nothing but the fantasies, the history of religion is disillusioning. Religion ordinarily asserts that her imaginings have objective existence, that the god, be it Isis or Apollo or Angra Mainyu, abides in the real world. Time and time again men learn that this claim does not correspond with fact; the human intellect eventually makes a clean sweep of all such fictitious objectivities. But religious fantasy is the bridge by which human beings, generation after generation, pass to a realization of the sacredness of community. Though the gods eventually dissolve like the figments of a dream, the evaluations which they symbolize seldom perish.

VI

Turning to these evaluations, we discover the fundamental similarity of the great living religions. Despite their particularistic creeds and rituals, they are a good deal alike in their moral injunctions, which exalt the widest human community. Precepts such as we associate with Christianity or Judaism occur in all the great scriptures. For example, among the aphorisms of Confucius we find: "Do not do unto others what you do not want others to do unto you." In the *Tao-te ching* of Lao-tsu we read: "Return love for great hatred." In an ancient Buddhist gospel we discover: "Cleanse your heart of malice and cherish no hatred, not even against your enemies, but embrace all living things with kindness." In a Hindu sacred book we are told: "As one's life is dear to himself, so also are those of all beings." In a Mohammedan text we read: "No one of you is a believer until he loves for his brother what he loves for himself." [11] The unity of outlook indicated by these typical passages is an immensely impressive fact—a refutation of the superficial relativism which emphasizes exclusively the differences among the peoples of the earth.

In thus generalizing the moral values of community, religion may appear to make an exaggerated or even nonsensical claim. For example, it may appear to be a meaningless paradox to say that even a stranger should be treated as a friend. Yet this paradox is at the very heart of the moral code of the higher religions. Of course, we cannot love strangers with the same personal intimacy that we feel towards friends. Love, nevertheless, *can* be projected beyond the intimate circle; it can become a very wide encompassing bond; it can become, in a sense, the basis of one's life and the supreme motivating force of one's being. Love of this sort is what Buddha had in mind when he said: "All the means that can be used as helps toward doing right avail not the sixteenth part of the emancipation of the heart through love." [12]

I do not deny that there is a darker side to religion. When human beings feel lonely and impotent and wretched, they may express their hatreds and frustrations in malign myths, such as the doctrine that the damned are everlastingly tortured by reason of man's sin and God's pleasure. A great many critics, from Xenophanes to Bertrand Russell and Morris Cohen, have exposed the fanaticism, cruelty, and superstition that have poisoned the well-springs of religious thought.

The effect of religion upon morality, moreover, has often been like that of an anodyne. Advancing the doctrine that the universe is the handiwork of a perfect and omnipotent God, it has maintained that all evil is eternally resolved into harmony.

[11] The quotations in this paragraph, in the order in which they occur, are from Lin Yutang, *The Wisdom of Confucius* (New York: Modern Library, 1938), p. 186; Robert O. Ballou, *The Portable World Bible*, p. 504; Paul Carus, *The Gospel of Buddha According to Old Records* (Chicago: Open Court, 1904), p. 106; Ballou, *The Portable World Bible*, p. 156; ibid., p. 1337.
[12] T. W. Rhys David, "Buddhism," *Encyclopaedia Britannica*, 11th ed. (Cambridge: Cambridge at the University Press, 1910), p. 744.

Instead of realizing the ideal, it has idealized the real. And even when it has been deeply concerned with human suffering, it has often been the victim of a serious illusion. This has been the notion that we should "save" men by spiritual conversion alone. To affirm spiritual *ends* and to neglect material *means*, to seek to change men's hearts without changing their circumstances, to proclaim "peace and justice" but to disregard the social causes of war and injustice, to put exclusive emphasis upon inner conversion and to discount the obstacles and opportunities of the external environment, is the main fallacy of traditional religious morality. It will not do to plead that goodness is a state of mind and that its physical embodiment is secondary and incidental—this is a profound error of principle, a false religious idealism. It neglects the constant interplay of mind and nature, spirit and matter, thought and things. Its idealism is morally futile or mischievous because it distracts men's attention from the brute material forces which, in the absence of scientific understanding and political control, are left to determine human destiny.

Substantial though these evils and illusions may be, they pervert and betray religion rather than express its innermost essence. If our interpretation is correct, this essence is the sense of sacredness based primarily upon the impulse of self-transcendence and communion. It is for us to separate the gold from the dross.

VII

I shall conclude with a few reflections upon the relation of faith to the great crisis of our age. History has now lent a new terrible urgency to the old, old question, "What shall we do to be saved?" Why has this come to pass? The deeper and more ultimate explanation is that an atom, elusive though it be, is more easily understood and controlled than a mind. In the development of humanity different functions reach maturity at different stages: the understanding and control of matter, being less complex, has reached maturity before the understanding and control of mind. Physical science, like a hare, has raced far ahead, whereas other human functions move tortoise-slow far in the rear. Mankind will not be out of danger until *art*, the impulse to appreciate, *religion*, the impulse to commune, *politics*, the impulse to govern, and *humanistic science*, the impulse to understand human nature, reach a maturity comparable to that of physical science and technology. When that time comes, men can safely unlock the ultimate energies of the universe.

But now, in the interval of mortal danger, what can we do? First, we must buy time, we must stave off catastrophe. The evil passions that incite to war—fear, hatred, intolerance, and lust for power—are probably more rampant in the Soviet East than in the West, but they exist to a very dangerous degree in both areas. A truly liberal religion can help to alleviate these passions. It can teach human beings to return love for hatred. It can awaken in men's minds the *hope* of the great community. It can penetrate the iron curtains of the human spirit by kindness and patient understanding. It can demonstrate, as the Quakers have done, that decency knows no boundaries of class or race or nation. Thereby it can play an invaluable role in preventing an atomic World War III.

Second, we must strive to bring the lagging human functions to maturity; and religion is one of these functions. Its coming of age cannot just be whistled for and produced to meet an emergency. The deepest tides of the human spirit flow slowly, and they answer no command. We cannot foresee in advance, moreover, the exact form that a mature religion will take. It will probably arise, little by little, with the creation of a new social order, and differ fundamentally from the old orthodoxies. It may find more adequate expression in art and literature than in public worship or theological creed.

Whatever form religion may take, it is unlikely to die out. Its value is not like that of a toy, the bauble of humanity's childhood, to be discarded as soon as our critical intellect matures. The religious impulse is as enduring as the human spirit itself—for it expresses the deep instinctive need to transcend selfhood and establish sympathetic relations to other things and especially to other spirits. All peoples and all ages feel this desire, and they cling to religion because it ministers, however crudely, to this impulse.

In our age of crisis, the need of self-transcendence is greater than ever before. The rise of an individualistic, technological, and industrialized civilization has undermined primary social relationships. The intimate unities of medieval life—the communal ties of family, gild, manor, neighborhood, and parish—have gradually been displaced by huge anonymous organizations and casual, fragmentary, dehumanized relationships. When life thus becomes impersonal and mechanically rationalized, men tend to lose the emotional basis of religion—the feeling of community. An industrialized mass-society, when undirected by humane social planning, notoriously tends toward a vulgar commercialistic materialism, or toward ugly forms of psychic regression, such as fascism. The main signs of crisis—ruthless competition, war, race hatred, political fanaticism, and tyranny—express the self-assertive and sadistic impulses which have now become marked. The very freedom that human beings have won at such prodigious cost is being threatened or destroyed by intolerance and aggression.

The supreme social problem of our age is to reconcile freedom and organization. Freedom without organization is a delusion: it spells anarchy and material bondage. Organization without freedom is a terrible straitjacket. But *free* organization—the spontaneous and uncoerced integration of the members of a society—is precisely what I mean by community. The spirit of community, I am convinced, must be given a new lease of life if we are happily to resolve the great crisis of our age. With patient, undaunted, stubborn persistence, we must create a world community to replace the anarchy of absolute nation-states, and we must renew the small, intimate, friendly community, without which the great community will lack roots and vitality. Step by step, we must build a new cooperative social order which will make the well-being of each citizen part of the well-being of all. Not only religion, but all the basic forms of human culture, must participate in this supreme task; but very little can be achieved unless there is strong conviction to lend to moral aspiration.

Even if I were gifted with all the capacities of a great seer, I could not in the brief time at my disposal sketch for you the new faith and scheme of values which we so urgently require. I can merely indicate my strong conviction that we must bring back, into the very heart of our culture, the sense of community which our impersonal and over-disciplined machine civilization has so largely sacrificed. We must disengage this spiritual jewel from the exaggerated and intemperate claims of an uncritical supernaturalism. Only thus can the spirit of community be made to shine in its true light.

I do not think it is necessary or desirable to cast wholly aside the old religious myths and symbols. We should not overlook the psychological fact that the concrete image, as in the story of Job or the vivid personality of Christ or Buddha, is more unforgettable and inspiring than the mere abstract precept. But the image should be interpreted in a new manner, not with the superstitious literalism of the fundamentalist, but with the ever-present realization of its ideal import and poetic substance. If we retain the old language, if we speak, for example, of "the brotherhood of man under the fatherhood of God," we should construe the ancient symbols in terms consistent with modern knowledge.

Likewise, if we continue to employ the concept of "God," we should interpret it in light of modern insights. We should have in mind a different sort of being than the traditional anthropomorphic divinity; ours must be the kind of God that is empirically discoverable: a finite, immanent, evolving, pluralistic God—the society of all the forces, human and natural, pushing on toward the good. Recent science and philosophy support the view that there *is* such a nisus, such an antientropic drive, toward richer quality and more inclusive unity. As we now envisage nature, it exhibits a series of levels of increasing complexity and wider integration: electrons, atoms, molecules, simple cells, plants, animals, personalities, and human communities form a mounting series. The higher levels tend to succeed the lower in time: there has been a progression from the amoeba to Neanderthal man, and from the very primitive level of human life to the greatest heroes, artists, thinkers, and saints. Each integrative level, moreover, exhibits its own emergent qualities and laws, and we must take account of the higher categories—the organic, qualitative, teleological, and social—in interpreting the more complex levels. There are biologists of repute, such as W. C. Allee, and anthropologists of distinction, such as Ashley Montagu, who maintain that the most important fact in organic evolution is cooperation—that without cooperation, without mutual aid, it is not possible to live and to advance. Likewise modern psychiatry has maintained that love is the key to life's riddles, and that when love is frustrated, the personality becomes disordered, morbid, and hostile.

These facts and conclusions do not mean that the universe *as a whole* is an organism, or a purposive mind, or is governed by a person, or forms a spiritual community. An idealistic interpretation of *all* reality may ultimately turn out to be correct, but upon the basis of our present knowledge, it would be very rash to assert it. But even if the material environment is not itself purposive, it has proved itself *fit* to produce purposive beings and the higher levels of value. Even if nature is not alive, it enables the development of fullness of life. Even if the universe is not a community, the ideal of fellowship is deeply based upon the nature of things.

I do not know how the universe will appear to a scientist several centuries from now. It may be that all our present insights are but the pale shadow of the reality yet to be revealed. It may be that existence is infinitely richer and finer than we have guessed, and that the future will be far more majestic than the past. It may be that all that is and has been is but the beginning of the beginning. We move through a little circle of light amid a deep night of mystery, and though modern science has widened the circle, it has deepened rather than dispelled our wonder and awe. Hope depends upon such realization of the "poetry of life," its depths, its mystery, its wonderful promise.

As human knowledge unfolds, the idea of community will find new unprecedented modes of expression; but it will have a profounder hold upon the human heart if men clearly realize that it is a fresh variation of man's ancient and fundamental religious intuition. The essential problem is to unite genuine feeling and tradition with modern forms of interpretation—to preserve the force of archaic religion while eliminating its obscurantism—to link new idioms and insights with the ancient poetic symbols of the race. Thus we can renew human faith without committing intellectual hara-kiri—we can achieve self-transcendence and the values of community while making a creative and humane use of the miraculous powers of science and technology.

Epilogue

Thoughts for a Time of Peril

The Greatest of Wonders

CHORUS:
Wonders are many on earth, and the greatest of these
Is man, who rides the ocean and takes his way
Through the deeps, through wind-swept valleys of perilous seas
    That surge and sway.

He is master of ageless Earth, to his own will bending
The immortal mother of gods by the sweat of his brow,
As year succeeds to year, with toil unending
    Of mule and plough.

He is lord of all things living; birds of the air,
Beasts of the field, all creatures of sea and land
He taketh, cunning to capture and ensnare
    With sleight of hand;

Hunting the savage beast from the upland rocks,
Taming the mountain monarch in his lair,
Teaching the wild horse and the roaming ox
    His yoke to bear

The use of language,the wind-swift motion of brain
He learnt; found out the laws of living together
In cities, building him shelter against the rain
    And wintry weather.

There is nothing beyond his power. His subtlety
Meeteth all chance, all danger conquereth.
For every ill he hath found its remedy,
    Save only death.

            Sophocles, *Antigone*, trans. by E. F. Watling

Even Babylon—That Proudest of Cities—Is Hurled Dow

Thus with violence shall that great city Babylon be hurled down,
and shall be found no more at all.
    And the voice of harpers, and musicians, and of pipers,
and trumpeters, shall be heard no more at all in thee;
    And no craftsman, of whatever craft he be, shall be found
any more in thee;
    And the sound of a millstone shall be heard no more at all in thee
    And the light of a candle shall shine no more at all in thee.
    And the voice of the bridegroom or of the bride
shall be heard no more at all in thee.
    For thy merchants were the great men of the earth;
    For by thy sorceries were all nations deceived.

                        Revelation 18:21-2

Scientific Warfare

It is not probable that war will ever absolutely cease until
science discovers some destroying force so simple in its admi-
nistration, so horrible in its effects, that all art, all gallantry,
will be at an end, and battles will be massacres which the
feeling of mankind will be unable to endure.

        W. Winwood Reade, *The Martyrdom of Man*, 1872

The Present Choice of Humankind

As geological time is reckoned, man has so far existed only for a very short period—1,000,000 years at the most. What he has achieved, especially during the last 6,000 years, is something utterly new in the history of the cosmos, so far at least as we are acquainted with it. For countless ages the sun rose and set, the moon waxed and waned, the stars shone in the night, but it was only with the coming of man that these things were understood. In the great world of astronomy and in the little world of the atom, man has unveiled secrets which might have been thought undiscoverable. In art and literature and religion, some men have shown a sublimity of feeling which makes the species worth preserving. Is all this to end in trivial horror because so few are able to think of man rather than of this or that group of men? Is our race so destitute of wisdom, so incapable of impartial love, so blind even to the simplest dictates of self-preservation, that the last proof of its silly cleverness is to be the extermination of all life on our planet?—for it will be not only men who will perish, but also the animals, whom no one can accuse of Communism or anti-Communism.

I cannot believe that this is to be the end. I would have men forget their quarrels for a moment and reflect that, if they will allow themselves to survive, there is every reason to expect the triumphs of the future to exceed immeasurably the triumphs of the past. There lies before us, if we choose, continual progress in happiness, knowledge, and wisdom. Shall we, instead, choose death, because we cannot forget our quarrels? I appeal as a human being to human beings: remember your humanity, and forget the rest. If you can do so, the way lies open to a new Paradise; if you cannot, nothing lies before you but universal death.

* Bertrand Russell, Portraits from Memory, 1956

Meditation on Life

A free man thinks of nothing less than of death, and his wisdom is not a meditation upon death but upon life.

Benedict Spinoza, *Ethics*, 1677

Index

Index

Communication: importance to community, 90, 91; and religion, 105
Community: meaning of, xii–xiii, 86–87, 88; truth within, 51; and art, 74; and individuality, 83; communication within, 90, 91; and religion, 109
Condorcet, Antoine, 78
Confucius; teachings of, related to Christianity, 115; mentioned, 51, 103, 112
Conklin, Edwin G., 45
Contextualistic method: as method of science, 51–52
Cresson, André, 45
Crisis: defined, xi; religion in age of, 118–19
Cromwell, Oliver, 103
Crow Indians: religion of, 109

Dadaists, 62
Darwin, Charles, 51, 103
Darwinism: applied to society, 44–45
David, Hans T., 68
de Chirico, Giorgio. See Chirico, Giorgio de
DeGaulle, General Charles, 14
de Gobineau, Joseph Arthur. See Gobineau, Joseph Arthur de
Descartes, René, 78, 103
Dewey, John: on meaning of community, xii, 87, 89, 92; advocacy of scientific method, 79, 82–83, 96; optimism of, 80, 95; *Art as Experience*, 81; *A Common Faith*, 81; and individual freedom, 84–85, 98; *Democracy and Education*, 90; mentioned, xiii, 47, 78
Dickens, Charles, 16
Dostoevsky, Feodor, 58
Drummond, Henry, 45
Dukas, Paul, 67
Durkheim, Emile, 107, 112

Eastman, Max, 68
Economics: unpredictability of, 11
Ehrlich, Paul, 11
Einstein, Albert, 12, 103, 104
Eliot, T. S., 58, 67
Elizabeth, Queen, 23
Ellul, Jacques, 7
Epicurus, 51

Faraday, Michael, 41
Feuerbach, Ludwig, xii
Florence: as cultural center, 103
France: during World War II, 30
Francis, Saint (Francis of Assisi), 112
Freedom, individual: related to community, 56, 84–85, 97–98
Freud, Sigmund, 3
Friendship: and community, 110–11
Fromm, Erich, 63
Futurists, 62

Galbraith, John Kenneth, 11
Galileo, Galilei, 41
Garibaldi, Giuseppe, 103
Geddes, Patrick, 45, 47
Gilgamesh, 115
Gobineau, Joseph Arthur de, 34
"God": modern concept of, 120
Government: role in individual freedom, 97–98
Great Schism: between art and humanities, 64, 66, 77
Greco-Roman civilization: breakdown of, 35
Greeks, ancient: religious community among, 106
Gropius, Walter, 66

Hegel, Georg: on interpretation of history, 34; *The Phenomenology of the Spirit*, 58; on alienation, 58
Hicks, Sir John, 11
Heilbroner, Robert L., 3
Heisenberg, Werner, 41
Hemingway, Ernest, 58
Herskovits, Melville, 32
Hinduism, 113
Hippocrates, 29
Hiroshima, 16, 30
Hitler, Adolf: invasion of France, 30; rise to power, 37; on Darwinist theory, 45; mentioned, 100
Holocaust, 6
Hobbes, Thomas: *Leviathan*, xiii; mentioned, 83
Honegger, Arthur: *Pacific 231*, 67
Huizinga, Jan, 24–25
Hulme, T. E., 59, 68
Humanities: schism with sciences, 77, 80–81

Index

Index

Orage, Alfred R., 30–31
Orpheus, 27
Ortega y Gasset, José, 68
Orwell, George: *1984*, 7, 84
Otto, Rudolf, 107

Page, Charles H., 93
"Pascal's Wager," 8
Pasteur, Louis, 103
Pericles, 23, 27, 103
Perry, Charles, 96
Personality types: effect of social organizations on, 63
Picasso, Pablo: *Woman in White*, 71, 75
Pittsburgh: pollution in, 16
Physics, quantum, 41
Plato: *Republic*, 101; *Apology*, 106; mentioned, 51, 103
Pope, Alexander, 41
Popper, Karl: on hazards of economic prophecy, 11–14; on modern communication, 105
Poussin, Nicolas, 71
Praxiteles, 103
Pythagoras, 51

Quakers, 118

Ransom, John Crowe, 72–73
Read, Herbert, 69–70
Relativity theory, 41
Religion: value of, 102–3, 116–17; and communication, 105, 106–7; and mysticism, 108, 113–14; and community, 109–11; relatedness of all sects, 115; future of, 118–19
Renaissance: art during, 60
Riesman, David, 63, 84
Rococo period, 69
Rome: Christianity in, 104
Roosevelt, President Franklin D., 12
Rousseau, Jean Jacques, 83
Rostovtzeff, Michael I., 35–36
Royce, Josiah: on the method of science, 49, 50; on community, 88–89, 111; mentioned, xii
Ruskin, John, 76
Russell, Bertrand, xiii, 116

Sartre, Jean-Paul: on individual freedom, 94; mentioned, 20–21, 58

Science: and technology, 12, 37, 40; as contextualistic method, 51–52; relationship between branches, 54–55; schism with art, 66, 77, 80–81
Seattle: pollution in, 16
Seidenberg, Roderick, 7
Shakespeare, William, 103
Shankara, 103
Shaw, George Bernard, 58
Shelley, Percy Bysshe: *Adonais*, 61
Shintoism: 107
Socrates, 66, 104
Socratic method, 51
Solitude: and religion, 109
Sophocles: *Oedipus the King*, 106
Soviet Union, 5
Sparta, 27
Spencer, Herbert, 46
Spengler, Oswald: on world future, 7, 79, 81; application of Darwinist theories, 45
Spinoza, Benedict, 103, 107
Stace, W. T.: *Religion and the Modern World*, 113; on mysticism and religion, 113–14
Stalin, Joseph, 100
Surrealists, 62

Taoism, 113
Technology: long-range consequences of, 13, 96
Thomson, John A., 45
Three Mile Island Nuclear Plant, 5
Thurber, James, 68
Tocqueville, Alexis de, 64
Tolstoy, Leo, 58, 107
Totalitarianism, 62
Totemism, 112
Toynbee, Arnold J.: theories on social crisis, 29–30; on class conflict, 35; mentioned, xi, 27
Truth: and community, 51

Urban environment: role of art in, 76
United States, 5

Valhalla, 115
Van Gogh, Vincent, 58, 61
Vasari, 61
Veblen, Thorstein: *The Theory of the Leisure Class*, 12; mentioned, 32, 47

[130]

Index

Vinci, Leonardo da, 78
Voltaire, 41

Wang Li (Chinese painter), 72
Warsaw: recovery from World War II, 16
Washington, Lake: pollution in, 16
Washington, University of, 65
Waste, excessive: as sign of social crisis, 33
Weisskopf, Victor F., 5
Wells, H. G.: on world's future, 6–7, 39, 79; on synthesis of world knowledge, 54; on community, 91; *The New Machiavelli*, 91; mentioned, 58
Wertheimer, Leo, 43
Whistler, James: "Ten O'Clock Lecture," 75

Whitehead, Alfred North: on religion, 102; on society as hierarchy, 111; mentioned, 47
Whitman, Walt: *Democratic Vistas*, 74; mentioned, 71, 108
Whyte, William, Jr., 63, 84, 91–92
Wilson, Colin: *The Outsider*, 58
Wordsworth, William: "Lines Composed near Tintern Abbey," 113, 114
Worringer, Wilhelm, 68
Wright, Frank Lloyd, 66, 96

Xenophanes, 116
Xerxes, 27

Yahweh, 115

Zarathustra, 103